F-100 SUPER SABRE AT WAR

THOMAS E. GARDNER

First published in 2007 by Zenith Press, an imprint of MBI Publishing Company, Galtier Plaza, Suite 200, 380 Jackson Street, St. Paul, MN 55101 USA

© Thomas E. Gardner, 2007

All rights reserved. With the exception of quoting brief passages for the purposes of review, no part of this publication may be reproduced without prior written permission from the Publisher.

Zenith Press titles are also available at discounts in bulk quantity for industrial or sales-promotional use. For details write to Special Sales Manager at MBI Publishing Company, Galtier Plaza, Suite 200, 380 Jackson Street, St. Paul, MN 55101 USA.

To find out more about our books, join us online at www.zenithpress.com.

Editor: Steve Gansen
Designer: James Kegley

Library of Congress Cataloging-in-Publication Data
Gardner, Thomas E., 1954-
  F-100 Super Sabre at war / by Thomas E. Gardner.
     p. cm.
  ISBN-13: 978-0-7603-2860-6 (softbound)
  ISBN-10: 0-7603-2860-9 (softbound)
  1. F-100 (Jet fighter plane)—History. I. Title.
  UG1242.F5G37 2007
  623.74'64—dc22
                               2006027123

Printed in China

On the cover, main: An F-100D s/n 55-3712 with 450-gallon external fuel tanks. *Lt. Col. T. Barnes via David W. Menard*

Inset: A quartet of 110th TFS Missouri Air National Guard Huns fly in formation over the Mississippi River. *Courtesy Jay Miller Aviation History Collection*

On the back cover: Two F-100Ds of the 110th TFS, Missouri Air National Guard, peel off to make a gunnery range pass. *Courtesy Jay Miller Aviation History Collection*

On the frontispiece: A four-ship formation of Texas Air National Guard F-100Ds cruises over their home state. *Courtesy Jay Miller Aviation History Collection*

On the title page: An F-100F s/n 56-3740 of the 131st Fighter Squadron (FS), Massachusetts Air National Guard, performs a low pass without its external fuel tanks, possibly indicating a test flight after extended maintenance. *Courtesy Jay Miller Aviation History Collection*

About the author
Thomas E. Gardner is a native of southern California. His enthusiasm for aircraft began as a young boy with a trip to Point Mugu Naval Air Station with his father to view the likes of the F4D-1 Skyray and Vought's immortal F-8 Crusader. He is a graduate of Bradley University in mechanical engineering and is pursuing a masters degree in aeronautical science at Embry-Riddle Aeronautical University. He lives in Peoria, Illinois, with his wife of twenty-one years and their four children.

CONTENTS

PREFACE		6
ACKNOWLEDGMENTS		7
CHAPTER ONE	ORIGIN OF THE "HUN"	8
CHAPTER TWO	F-100 FEATURES	20
CHAPTER THREE	FLIGHT TEST	34
CHAPTER FOUR	F-100 MODELS	52
CHAPTER FIVE	WEAPONS SYSTEMS	62
CHAPTER SIX	OPERATORS WORLDWIDE	76
CHAPTER SEVEN	F-100F WILD WEASEL	82
CHAPTER EIGHT	F-100B/F-107A: THE OTHER "HUN"	90
APPENDICES		
A: SPECIFICATIONS		102
B: PRODUCTION LIST		105
C: MODELER'S SECTION		106
D: SIGNIFICANT DATES		115
INDEX		126

PREFACE

The North American F-100 Super Sabre was truly a revolution in aircraft design. It was not only America's first supersonic fighter, but in fact, the first in the world. The Super Sabre preempted the Soviet Union from being first into the supersonic arena with the MiG-19 by nearly five months.

The F-100 would soon establish many firsts in its long, distinguished career. It was the first operational jet fighter to exceed Mach 1 in level flight. It was the first in a noble line of fighters soon to be known as the "Century Series." Its stable mates would include the Convair F-102 Delta Dagger, Lockheed F-104 Starfighter, Republic F-105 Thunderchief, and the venerable Convair F-106 Delta Dart. The F-100 also established numerous speed and altitude records in its heyday.

But the Super Sabre was not without its flaws. It was discovered rather late in its flight test program that the F-100 suffered from design deficiencies, which led to the dangerous phenomenon known as "inertia coupling." Because the concept of "concurrent engineering" was being embraced at the time, several production lots designated F-100A were already delivered and deployed to a few leading air force squadrons before the bugs were worked out of the radical plane's design. This dire problem of inertia coupling was quickly overcome, and field modifications were made to existing aircraft allowing the F-100 to continue life in the C, D, and F variants.

Nearly all who flew or maintained the F-100 loved it. It would soon earn the nickname "Hundert," or more affectionately, the "Hun."

The Skyblazers were the aerobatic team of USAF Europe from 1956 to 1961. *Courtesy Jay Miller Aviation History Collection*

ACKNOWLEDGMENTS

I would like to take this opportunity to thank the following individuals whose selfless contributions helped in the completion of this book: Alan Renga of the San Diego Aerospace Museum; Jill Schaefer of Thomson's Aviation Manuals; Ken Dayer of the Arkansas Aerospace Education Center; Jack Connors, retired engineer and archivist at Pratt & Whitney Aircraft Engines; Ken Quimby of the Arkansas Aerospace Education Center; Janet Koonce of City Blue Technologies; Joyce Best, who I know spent countless hours deciphering my handwriting; and, most of all, to David Menard whose guidance and discerning eye significantly contributed to this book's authenticity and completion. Lastly, to my wife Susan, whose constant encouragement kept me from going crazy.

YF-100 s/n 52-5754 flying high over Southern California. Its vertical stabilizer was later shortened, leading to instability problems and, ultimately, to the accident that killed test pilot George Welch. *Courtesy David W. Menard*

CHAPTER ONE

ORIGIN OF THE "HUN"

DEVELOPMENTAL HISTORY

North American Aviation (NAA) by the end of 1948 was the preeminent manufacturer of superb military aircraft in the free world. It had produced stunningly successful aircraft, such as the World War II P-51 Mustang and its successor, the F-86 Sabre. Lee Atwood, president of North American at that time, arrived at several fundamental and decisive conclusions. First, the time was right for North American to proceed in the company's evolution in fighter aircraft design. Moreover, this time they were going supersonic. Secondly, a powerplant would soon be available to enable a fighter to exceed Mach 1 in level flight. Third, these goals were attainable—especially with the influx of technology occurring at that time. Advanced aerodynamic research captured from German aircraft companies like Arado, Heinkel, Messerschmitt, and Focke-Wulfe during the waning days of World War II, combined with recent research conducted by the National Advisory Committee on Aeronautics (NACA), convinced Atwood that a supersonic fighter was not only attainable, but also necessary.

On 3 February 1949, Raymond H. Rice, North American Aviation's vice president of engineering, gave his blessing to his top engineers to begin to explore the possibilities of achieving supersonic flight with the firm's newly developed F-86 Sabre fighter. Bear in mind that the sound barrier had been broken a scant year and a half earlier by U.S. Air Force (USAF) Captain Charles E. Yeager in the Bell XS-1. Scientists knew relatively little about the so-called "wall in the sky" and next to nothing about sustained supersonic flight. The German aeronautical research, captured war booty, was of significant help. Still, large-scale supersonic wind tunnels were hard to come by, and this hampered the effort. Unencumbered by these deficiencies, NAA pressed on with its first study, increasing the existing Sabre's wing to a 45-degree sweep angle. Studies further indicated that increasing the sweep angle and modifying the fuselage did little to enhance performance. The problem was that as the aircraft approached transonic and then and supersonic speeds, drag forces acting on the aircraft would increase substantially, thus requiring an inordinate amount of power.

Rice knew that in order to obtain speeds in the realm of Mach 1 and beyond, a powerful axial-flow turbojet would be required. During the initial stages of the conceptualization of the F-100's design, the only powerplants available of notable power and reliability were of the centrifugal type with double-sided compressors, namely the Pratt & Whitney J48, whose classic lines were sculpted in accordance to the earlier Whittle/Rover/Rolls-Royce designs. This type of engine was simply out of the question. It had a rather robust cross-section much too large to install into a thoroughbred fighter whose fineness ratio—the proportion of the width to the length of the fuselage—had to be kept to a minimum. There was, of course, the Westinghouse J40 that was then under development for the Douglas F4D-1 Skyray navy fighter. Eventually, this engine proved troublesome and unreliable, consistently plagued with compressor stalls, surges, and broken blades that spelled the demise of the entire powerplant—and, eventually, Westinghouse's future as a jet engine manufacturer. There was also the General Electric XJ53, developed specifically for supersonic flight. This proved much too large and complex to operate in a fighter.

The Allison Division of General Motors was the first to offer a realistic powerplant for the F-86 redesign. This would take form in a reworked J35 turbojet whose basic design elements came from a General Electric Company design. Apparently Allison acquired it and revamped it to produce 9,000 pounds of continuous thrust, double the output of the GE J47 powering front-line Sabres at that time. In August 1949, General Electric proposed an advanced J47 producing 9,400 pounds of continuous thrust, augmented by a relatively new concept known as afterburning. The latter would produce a total thrust output of 13,000 pounds.

It was at this point that the engineers decided that the F-86D Sabre Dog, an all-weather interceptor version of the F-86, was best suited for operating in the transonic flight regime. On 14 September 1949, the engineers infused new life as well as enthusiasm into the design studies centering on the advanced J47. Early calculations predicted a performance envelope of Mach 1.03 in level flight at 35,000 feet altitude.

What finally transpired through the culmination of all the previous design studies were three important final design phases: The first was an advanced F-86D. This was reflected in an unsolicited proposal to the U.S. Air Force (Report NA-50-859), initiated on 25 August 1950. This design reflected North American's persistence with the 45-degree wing sweep angle accompanied by a relatively new concept of an area-ruled fuselage. The air force rejection only strengthened North American's resolve with Phase 2.

Phase 2 was an advanced F-86E, retaining, like its predecessor the F-86D, its wings, tail, and powerplant, only offering a redesigned, slimmer fuselage and front inlet. This, too, the air force rejected.

Undaunted, North American presented the U.S. Air Force with Phase 3 on 14 May 1951. This design was the embodiment of both the F-86D and F-86E features, still embracing the 45-degree sweptback wing.

On 19 January 1951, the Super Sabre began life in the guise of an in-house study called "Sabre 45." The number 45 referred to the wings' sweep angle located along its leading edge. North American Aviation entirely funded this study, with the exception of the development of a suitable powerplant for the Super Sabre. In this area, the U.S. Air Force's influence was quite evi-

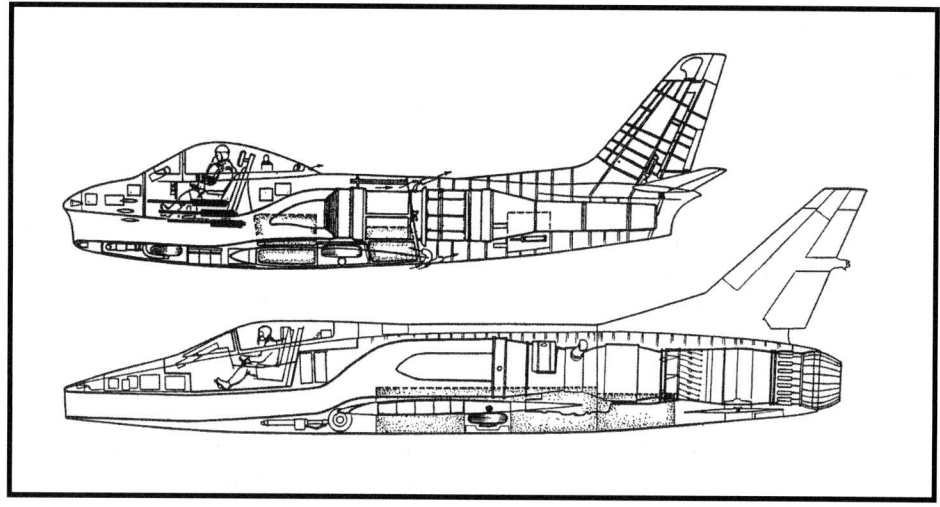

The comparative sizes of the F-86E Sabre and the YF-100 are evident in this illustration. Notice the size difference in ducting between both aircraft.
Courtesy Jay Miller Aviation History Collection

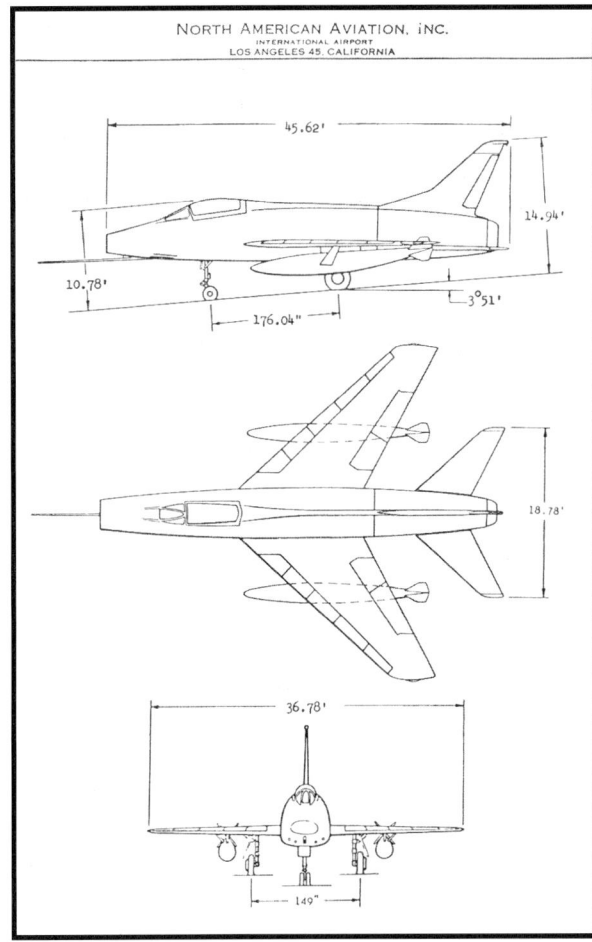

This is a drawing of the finalized Sabre 45 product named Super Sabre. These are the relative overall dimensions of the YF-100. *Courtesy Thomson's Aviation Manual*

compressor stall, surge, or blade fracturing due to high residual stresses on the turbine blades. This arrangement also provided better fuel economy and higher power. Pratt & Whitney's J57 redefined turbojet design, enhanced reliability, and insured a quantum leap in efficiency. In order to enhance power output, an afterburner was added to boost the J57 to 14,000 pounds of thrust. Well over 20 feet long, 42 inches in diameter, and weighing over 5,000 pounds, the J57-P-7 was finally selected to power the Hun. This left no doubt in Rice's mind that the Sabre 45 could exceed Mach 1.

On 14 May 1951, North American Aviation submitted a proposal to the U.S. Air Force for the construction of two Sabre 45 prototype air superiority fighters, in order to speed up delivery of production units for combat use. On 1 November 1951, the U.S. Air Force issued letter contract AF 33 (600)-6545 authorizing the production of two Sabre 45 prototypes. Also located in the heart of the contract were provisions for further engineering design, fabrication of production tooling, and the procurement of long-lead time materials and equipment to build approximately ninety-four Sabre 45 fighters.

The next step in the finalization of the Sabre 45 project was a mock-up inspection of the Sabre 45 prototype, which was completed on 9 November 1951. Finally, the U.S. Air Force officially designated the in-house study nicknamed Sabre 45 as F-100A on 7 December 1951.

Even with the air force's contract acceptance of the Sabre 45, it was apparent to NAA's engineering staff that the future aircraft still required some much-

dent, particularly in the area of financial support to Pratt & Whitney, whose legendary J57 would soon power the Hun.

The Pratt & Whitney J57 was a technological achievement in itself. What made its design so unique lay in a two-shaft, dual-rotor, two-spool or split compressor. A low-pressure turbine located behind the combustor powered the lower-pressure compressor. In addition, similarly, a high-pressure turbine powered the high-pressure compressor. The low-pressure compressor and turbine shaft were located inside the high-pressure compressor and turbine shaft, and each rotated at different angular velocities.

As complicated as it appeared, it actually was functionally quite simple. This definitive design concept promised greater compression ratios without

A photo of YF-100 s/n 52-5754 taken in April 1953, about a month prior to her first test flight. Notice the protective coating on the clamshell canopy. *USAF via David W. Menard*

YF-100 shipment no. 1 performs taxi tests on the dry lake bed at Edwards Air Force Base, California. *Courtesy Jay Miller Aviation History Collection*

The second YF-100 s/n 52-5755 sporting underwing ordnance makes a low pass for the photographer during takeoff. *Courtesy Jay Miller Aviation History Collection*

needed refinements. After the acceptance, North American issued an internal document outlining specific design deficiencies soon to be addressed. They included the reshaping of the fuselage to improve further its fineness ratio, extension of the clamshell canopy, and lowering the horizontal stabilizer below the chord plane of the wing. The USAF accepted all of these improvements on 23 June 1952.

Wind tunnel tests conducted by NACA revealed that the F-100, in its current design configuration, would not meet the projected speed of Mach 1.3 in level flight. More refinement was required. North American Aviation engineers initiated three significant design changes in their new fighter. The first was a thinning of the inlet lip to a finer edge to improve inlet flow, thus delivering higher-energy air to the engine. Second, engineers lengthened the nose by nine inches, further improving the fineness ratio through decreasing drag. Lastly, they reduced the thickness/chord (t/c) ratio by 50 percent for the horizontal and vertical stabilizers. The new t/c ratio would be 3.5 percent. When these improvements were completed, they had significant influence of what would later be experienced when flight-testing the Hun.

DESIGN

The F-100A Super Sabre was a high-speed, low-wing, air-superiority fighter capable of speeds in excess of Mach 1 in level flight. Its principal armaments were four T-130 20mm cannons. The F-100 had many outstanding features, one being its thin, 45-degree sweptback wings of moderate aspect ratio. Inboard ailerons, coupled with automatic leading-edge slats, further defined the sculpted wing possessed by the Hun.

The 45-degree sweep angle, which truly defined the Super Sabre from all the others, was the metamorphosis of design elements embodied in the wing and appendage of the F-86 Sabre fighter. Starting with the Sabre's wing sweep of 35 degrees and 10 percent airfoil thickness, the Hun was given a 45-degree sweep and a razor-thin wing of 7 percent thickness. Though the Super Sabre's wings were strong as well as stiff, the decision to locate the plane's ailerons more inboard than was common was a wise one. Previously, wing failures on other jets had been the result of aileron reversal and wing warping due to the aileron's outboard position along the trailing edge of the wing. Locating the ailerons at a more inboard station greatly reduced wing twist and bending, and significantly enhanced the Hun's rate of roll to 200 degrees per second at Mach 1.

The Super Sabre's leading-edge slats would extend and retract automatically, depending on what kind of aerodynamic forces were dominant during a particular phase of flight. The leading-edge slats increased maximum lift during takeoff and, they also delayed and limited wing buffet during flight. This allowed higher Gs to be incurred in diving turns and improved the lateral control characteristics of the aircraft as it approached stalling speed. It also permitted much higher constant altitude turns for certain speeds and engine power settings.

Another notable design feature was the F-100's finely tailored fuselage, being of high fineness ratio incorporating its highly efficient oval air inlet. This duct added 50 knots to the Super Sabre's total overall speed. Located roughly at midsection of the fighter was the heart and soul of the Hun, the Pratt & Whitney J57-P-7 engine. This is what gave the Hun its virility.

The longitudinal control of the F-100 was facilitated by the movement of the entire horizontal stabilizer, or more commonly known as, simply, a stabilator. It was located below the wing chord plane on the lower portion of the aft fuselage. This particular location placed the stabilator in a favorable wing-downwash area and eliminated the "pitch-up" effect encountered during pullup maneuvers in the transonic and supersonic regime. It is of particular note that the Bell XS-1 utilized this form of control in order to deal with oscillations of the plane near supersonic speed.

The flight control system of the F-100 utilized hydraulic power to the pressure of 3,000 psi (pounds per square inch). This system operated all the control surfaces. It is interesting to note that the ailerons and the horizontal stabilizer were actuated by two totally independent hydraulic systems, each system being of equal

The second production F-100A lifts off the runway in full afterburner. Notice its extended leading-edge wing slats in operation. *Courtesy David W. Menard*

power. Both systems were mounted in tandem so if one system failed the other would take over completely. The rudder was actuated by hydraulic power from the utility system. In the event of total hydraulic failure, the pilot could access control of the craft through a myriad system of cables, bell cranks, and pushrods.

North American engineers designed the control system to have what was called artificial feel during flight, so the pilot could not overfly the F-100 beyond its stressed structural limits. This was achieved by the use of spring bungees that pushed or pulled against the control yoke and rudder pedals while in use. Fixed at the end of each spring bungee was an attachment to the plane's structure via a trim actuator, while the moveable end was attached to a valve arm that pushed or pulled against the control yoke or pedals as they were applied.

The utility hydraulic system also supplied power for the normal operation of the landing gear. The landing gear wheel brakes, emergency brake accumulator, speed brake, gun purge, nose-wheel steering, and ram-air turbine were all also operated from the utility hydraulic system. The F-100 had retractable tricycle landing gear incorporating air-oil oleo struts accommodated with segmented rotor-type disk brakes mounted on the wheel axles accompanied by high-pressure pneumatic tires.

The Super Sabre utilized both direct and alternating electric power systems. For communication and navigation use, the Hun was equipped with an AN/ARC-34 UHF air-to-air or air-to-ground radio set. The Super Sabre also used an AN/ARN-6 radio compass accompanied with an AN/APX-6 identification radar.

The air conditioning and pressurization system maintained the cockpit environment. Heated or cooled air was channeled to the cockpit through air taken from the engine compressor and passed through a primary heat exchanger to the refrigeration unit. Here, the air was mixed to the exact temperature consistency chosen by the pilot. Pressurization control maintained a constant pressure differential of 2.75 psi from altitudes ranging between 21,200 to 31,000 feet. Above 31,000 feet, a constant pressure differential of 5 psi was maintained.

MANUFACTURING

The manufacturing of the F-100A would be strongly influenced by the Cook-Craigie Plan. This plan was a method of aircraft development conceived by Generals

YF-100 s/n 52-5754 in landing configuration minus a tail bumper. Take note of its novel speed brake, fully extended for enhanced speed control. *USAF via David W. Menard*

The fourth production F-100A carries pylons being used to determine which ordnance items could be carried safely. Notice the large vertical stabilizer used and a drogue chute deployed for added stopping power. *Courtesy Jay Miller Aviation History Collection*

Orval R. Cook and Laurence C. Craigie following World War II. Rather than build and test a series of prototypes before manufacturing the tooling and jigs to construct production aircraft, the Cook-Craigie Plan reversed the process and began with building the tooling and jigs and fabricating prototypes. If the prototypes performed well, production followed, but if the prototypes failed to fly as expected, the jigs had to be dismantled and rebuilt at great cost. This plan was in accordance with a newly developed discipline known as concurrent engineering, where the weapons system, in this case, the F-100, was developed simultaneously with the tooling, production, and training to run the Hun. This philosophy soon was proven flawed because of the F-100's vulnerability to inertia roll coupling discovered later in its flight-testing.

Manufacturing operations of the first YF-100 (52-5754) officially began in January 1952, with the primary emphasis being placed upon its tooling. The first prototype YF-100A was completed on 24 April 1953. The plane was test flown on 25 May 1953 and subsequently accepted by the air force on 30 June that same year. This was followed by a second YF-100, which in turn the U.S. Air Force accepted on 31 July 1953.

The primary manufacturing site for the F-100A was located at the North American Aviation Plant next to the Los Angeles International Airport. As the program and aircraft matured, a second production facility was required. In September 1954, a second production site was established at North American's Columbus, Ohio, plant. Here, upon contract authorization from the air force, 25 F-100Cs and 221 F-100Ds were to be produced.

The F-100, unlike the F-86, required more precision manufacturing techniques simply because it was a totally new, complex, and revolutionary aircraft. The F-100 operated at low, sustained supersonic speeds, which caused high structural and thermodynamic stresses. This called for a more robust design, which culminated in a more challenging and innovative manufacturing process.

Because of the inordinately closer tolerances required to produce the F-100 than previous jets, greater attention was paid in particular to the variations in temperature throughout the manufacturing sites. These slight differences did, in fact, affect the material dimensions, thus hampering the accuracy of a machined part that particular day. To resolve this problem, better temperature controls in areas especially reserved for the production of particular parts were maintained along with special handing procedures. Because of the nature and complexity of these many parts, manufacturing required seemingly endless amounts of machining operations, which were performed on vastly more complex machine tools.

In the manufacturing of the wing, maintaining a maximum thickness/chord ratio of 7 percent required the F-100's longerons and ribs to be machined from aluminum plate extending up to 1 3/4 inches in thickness. These components were then machined to a taper, which was performed on large horizontal milling machines, which operated in tandem.

The F-100A was the first aircraft to incorporate titanium in its initial design phase. It used roughly six times more titanium than its predecessor, the F-86D.

North American virtually pioneered many of the accepted titanium manufacturing and fabrication processes still in use in the aerospace industry today. All manufacturing schedules were met except during the in-field retrofitting needed to resolve the F-100A's tendency for inertia roll coupling.

The U.S. Air Force was not the only branch of the military interested in supersonic flight. The U.S. Navy displayed a keen interest as well. The Douglas Aircraft Company, under the guiding hand of its legendary designer, Ed Heinemann, explored the realm of transonic flight by developing the D-558-1 Skystreak under the auspices of the navy. The navy was also embroiled in supersonic research as well.

One of the more pressing disadvantages for carrier aircraft was the limited takeoff and landing space dictated by the available deck length of the aircraft carriers at that time. Compared to the rather generous runway lengths afforded to air force pilots, navy pilots operated their aircraft under totally different, and often divergent, circumstances. Air force pilots did not have to negotiate landings on heaving carrier decks often oscillating as much as four feet in the vertical and at night as well.

The inherent and differing operational climates significantly influenced the very nature of the aircraft design. Naval aircraft requirements called for high power-to-weight ratios, the highest of structural integrity, ease of maintenance, and resistance to salt-air corrosion. Naval aircraft, especially jets, were woefully underpowered, so saving weight became of great importance. Consequently, air force jets were often heavier and guided by totally different design criteria.

In May 1945, after Germany's unconditional surrender, two Douglas Aircraft Company aerodynamicists, A. M. O. Smith and Gene Root, were sent to Paris, France. Their immediate task was to assess captured German aerodynamic data and especially that of famed aircraft designer Dr. Alexander Lippisch. His expertise lay in the research of tailless aircraft culminating in the famed Messerschmitt Me-163 rocket-propelled interceptor. Smith and Root acquired a treasure trove of wind tunnel test data as well.

The Douglas Aircraft Company, notably Ed Heinemann, valued Dr. Lippisch's research and explored this concept of the tailless delta configuration. A delta wing would offer greater aerodynamic efficiencies at higher mach numbers and held great design promise, even with the utilization of existing low-powered turbojets.

Three pilots of the 479th FDW walk to their respective F-100As on the George Air Force Base flight line located in California. *Courtesy Jay Miller Aviation History Collection*

On 17 June 17 1947, the U.S. Navy Bureau of Aeronautics (BUAER), upon inspection of several proposals submitted by leading U.S. aircraft companies, selected the Douglas entry. Designated D-571 and drawn up by R. G. Smith, it was essentially a straight delta flying wing sporting a vertical stabilizer, paying credence to some advances in German jet fighters that never made it past the design stage. Eventually, the design evolved into the D-571-4, incorporating a smaller, rounded-off, blended delta-wing fuselage configuration. The navy became rather smitten with its overall appeal and awarded Douglas a contract for two prototypes on 16 December 1949. It was dubbed the XF4D-1 Skyray due to its manta ray–like appearance.

Meanwhile, the Soviets were actively developing their own supersonic designs, culminating in the MiG-19.

F-100As are being assembled on the production line. Notice the sign in the foreground, "Quality must be built into a product, it cannot be inspected into it." *USAF via David W. Menard*

The Farmer, as it was eventually known to the West by many reports and studies, would become the Super Sabre's rival. Although designed and configured very differently than the Super Sabre, it would fare none the better in performance, and the victor in a would-be dogfight would be the most skilled pilot.

All three aircraft, the F-100, F4D-1, and MiG-19, were designed employing semi-monocoupe stressed-skin construction. During the brief span of time that these aircraft were developed, quantum leaps in technology were commonplace, and in particular in the area of aircraft structures. Bear in mind that a scant five years earlier, World War II was ending and the pinnacle of fighter technology resided in piston-engine, propeller-driven aircraft that could not exceed 500 miles per hour in a dive. The advent of the turbojet enabled aircraft to shed their propellers, sweep their wings, and eventually exceed Mach 1 in level flight.

The ultimate load factors of fighters had not changed much in the five years since the end of World War II. The prominent fighter dominating that era was the North American P-51 Mustang, and this aircraft was stressed to a robust 12 Gs. As the flight envelope expanded, so did the overall speeds of the aircraft. Because of this fact, the overall wing thickness ratios decreased significantly to reduce drag, especially at high transonic speeds, therefore reducing the wing weight and structural integrity, or so it was thought. Sweeping the wings also introduced greater structural span than that of a straight wing employing the same area and aspect ratio.

Advances in metallurgical technology initiated an improvement in an increase of higher local working stresses, especially in compression, allowing higher wing skin loadings in the overall structure. This was the prevailing trend during this period in aircraft development.

World War II aircraft structures were fabricated in essence by wrapping relatively thin structural skins over an internal framework. Thicker skins were eventually needed to satisfy the new design paradigm incorporated in jet aircraft technology in the coming decades. This requirement was met through pre-forming, by rolling, augmented later through strengthened forming. Because thicker skins were being employed, internal webs rather than stiffness in the form of stringers were required, making riveting extremely difficult. Thus, it was necessary to develop new fabrication techniques. As a result, the art of machining became the preferred production method, especially in its use in tapering the thickness of components when required. Integral construction was also embraced by the early to mid-1950s, forming the webs and stringers to the skins as one unit.

Aerodynamic flutter, which is the rapid resonance of a wing or horizontal stabilizer when the applied aerodynamic loads meet the natural harmonic frequency of the wing or tail, often led to deadly results, becoming more frequent in occurrence. Wing torsion became paramount in design studies at that time. This was of great concern for North American engineers when designing the 45-degree wing of the Super Sabre. Designing an efficient aileron, which would not impose inordinate wing twist or deflection, was a challenge for them at best. They eventually solved the problem by designing a control that applies a rolling movement without twisting the wing: in essence, a control that applies an increment of lift to the center of pressure of the wing instead of its trailing edge. Spoilers rather than ailerons were eventually accepted as a possible solution to this dilemma and utilized in North American's F-107 design.

The Skyray, on the other hand, did not encounter this problem, due in part to its delta wings' geometry. The delta configuration allowed for adequate thickness, shorter span, and high wing area, which also invited higher wing loading. The blended wing/fuselage juncture afforded a more efficient overall structural design at the least possible weight. The blended wing/fuselage fillet also served to distribute the very large wing loads around the engine via multiple V-shaped spars. An item of particular note is that Ed Heinemann achieved his legendary status as a gifted designer due in part to his passion for eliminating excessive weight from his aircraft designs. In his quest to minimize structural weight in his XF4D-1 design, the outer skin panels were fabricated from very thin .0025–.0030-inch light aluminum alloy sheet. Any necessary stiffening was facilitated through a "pillowed" or double corrugated reinforced panel secured on the inside by spot welding. This provided panels that were very light, stable, and resistant to buckling.

The Skyray and the Super Sabre also shared the same powerplant, the Pratt & Whitney J57 afterburning turbojet. Initially, the Skyray was designed around the Westinghouse J40. As the story goes, the XF4D-1 was built way before the J40 was even pursuing its bench trials, thus establishing a dilemma. An Allison J35 was substituted instead until the cranky and unpredictable J40 was cleared for testing. Displaying amazing self-control, the navy was patient and remained a steadfast ally to Westinghouse. Eventually the J40 was cleared for use, but with disastrous results. The engine was not reliable and was linked to several crashes involving the McDonnell F-3H-1 Demon. As time passed, so did the navy's patience in regards to the J40. The J57 was soon approved for use in the Skyray and, due to Ed Heinemann's foresight in affording extra room in the Skyray's design as a hedge to accept other turbojets being developed in the event the J40 failed, the program was saved.

The Soviets' thoroughbred, the MiG-19, counterpart to the Super Sabre, went through seemingly endless prototypes, starting with the SM-1/2 (1-360 prototype) and ending with the SM-9/1. On 17 February 1954, even before the final conclusion to SM-9/1 testing occurred, the Council of Ministers and the Central Committee of the Communist Party issued Directive No. 286-133 ordering this vehicle into production under service designation MiG-19.

Several prototypes tested culminating into the production MiG-19 were reported to have gone supersonic, but it was the YF-100 that was the world's first production supersonic fighter, and North American was steadfast in its design resolution from its original inception as in-house project Sabre 45. The MiG-19 in some ways was akin to the Super Sabre in design relevance. Both operated with front air intakes, both incorporated highly swept wings, but here is where the similarities ended.

The MiG-19 incorporated a wing sweep angle of 55 degrees at quarter chord, 10 degrees higher than that of the Super Sabre. It also maintained a healthy adheral of 4.5 degrees, foreign to the F-100. The MiG-19 also required the combined power of two Klimov RD-9B turbojets each producing 7,165 pounds/3,250 kilograms with full afterburner. The Super Sabre only required the effort from one afterburning Pratt & Whitney J57-P-7 turbojet. The MiG possessed a slight edge in speed, but suffered unmercifully from the RD-9B's temperamental and unrelenting unreliability.

The MiG-19 was constructed employing a semi-monocoque structure. The forward fuselage bore a stark resemblance to its SM-2 and SM-9/1 cousins, up to and including frame 20. It also possessed a detach-

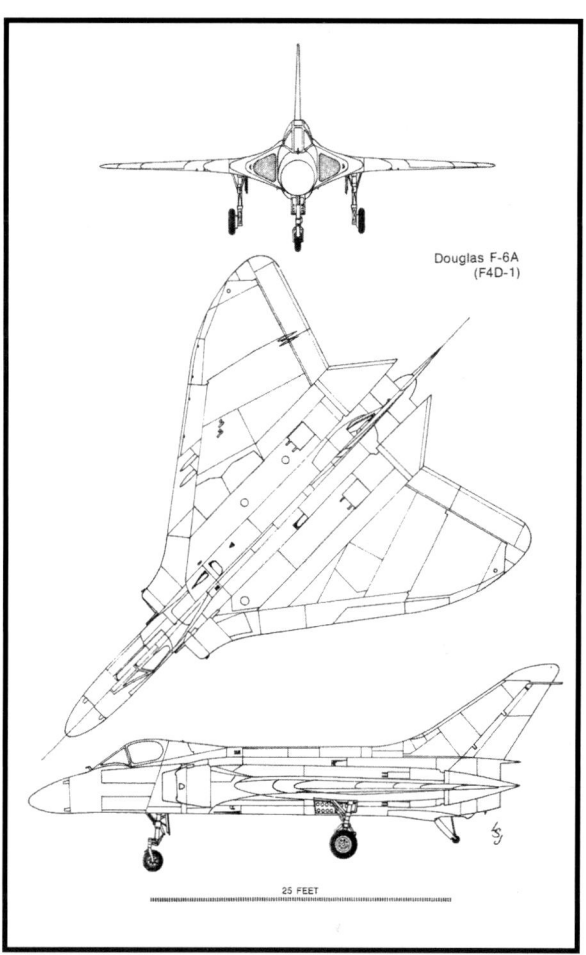

Unlike its other supersonic counterparts, the F4D-1 Skyray sported a delta tailless design. Douglas Aircraft designer Ed Heinman indulged in a totally different approach amidst the influx of changing technology in the U.S. Navy's quest to exceed Mach 1.
Courtesy San Diego Aerospace Museum

able rear fuselage, for ease of engine installation, a design feature shared with the Super Sabre.

The wings featured Tsagi flaps accompanied by and incorporating the use of a single boundary layer fence positioned mid span on each wing. The wing structure was composed largely of Elektron magnesium alloy castings and V95 aluminum alloy.

The MiG-19 also featured a tail unit possessing a conventional swept-tail layout. Fin sweep resided at 56 degrees quarter chord, while vertical tail area sported a generous 47.65 square feet, accented by two ventral fins canted 45 degrees outboard. The horizontal stabilizer was swept 55 degrees quarter chord and incorporated a

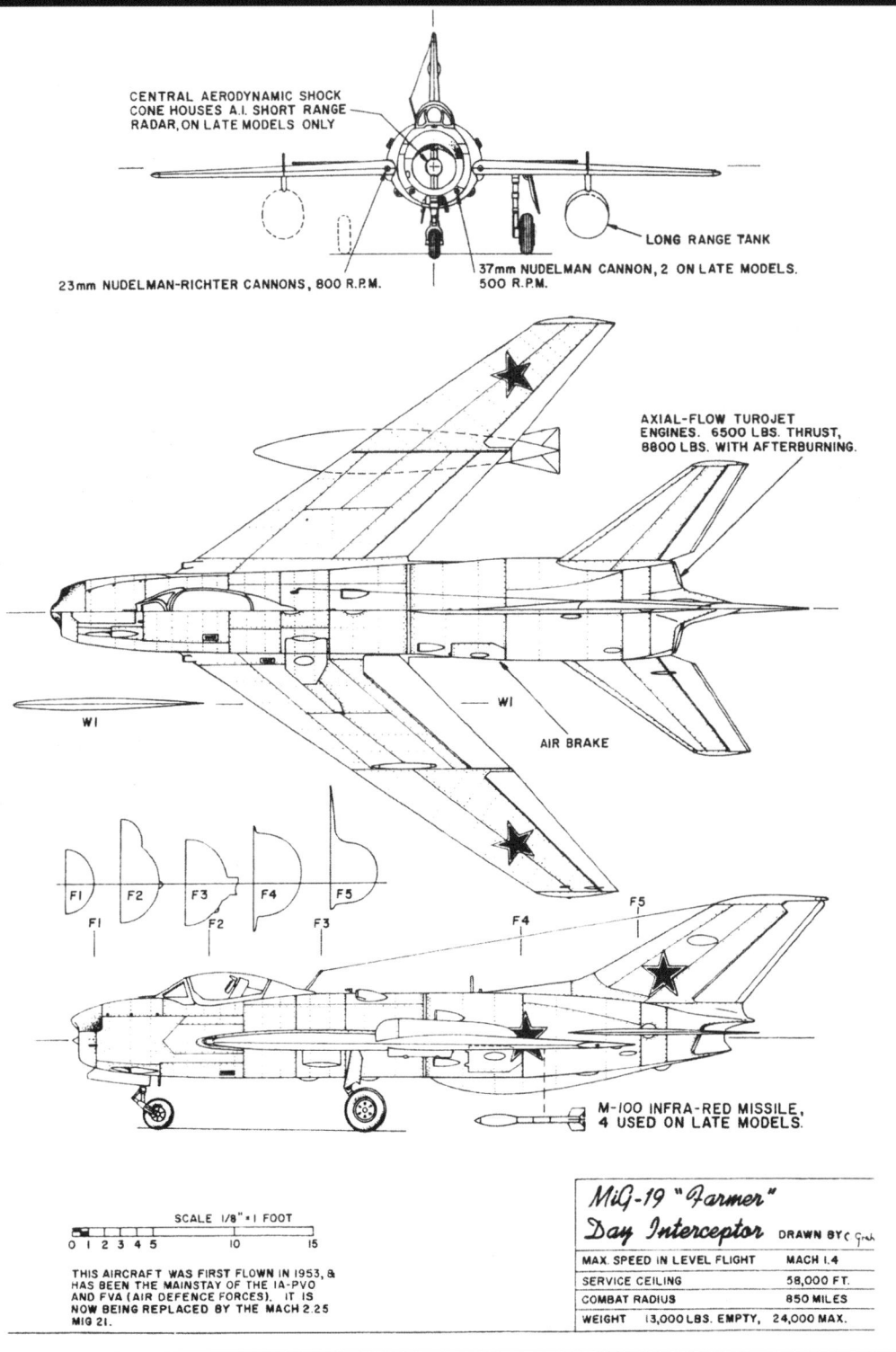

The MiG-19, fairly straightforward in design, appears to involve area ruling in its fuselage. In fact, the widening of the aft structure was necessary to accommodate the two Klimov RD-93 turbojets mounted side by side.
Courtesy San Diego Aerospace Museum

A Skyray of VF(AW)-3 in flight over NAS North Island, circa 1959. *Courtesy San Diego Aerospace Musuem*

Notice the smooth aerodynamic features possessed by the Skyray. Also, take note of the triangular side intakes, efficient enough to channel the airflow to its powerful J57 engine. *Courtesy San Diego Aerospace Museum*

horizontal tail area of 37.31 square feet. The stabilizer was positioned above the wing/fuselage centerline, unlike the Super Sabre's stabilizer arrangement. This led to some major stability problems during flight-testing of the MiG-19. This was due in part to the irregular airflow around its rear fuselage, resulting in supersonic flow in some areas, while other areas remained subsonic. This was later remedied by designing a cleaner tail fairing stabilizing the flow in that region.

The MiG-19 encountered many design problems as well as challenges. One problem posing considerable anxiety was how to achieve the desired structural integrity locating the wing at a low or mid position on the fuselage. Another problem dealt with adequate airflow in the ducts designed to pass the cockpit and feeding its two engines.

Some early MiG-19s had the nasty tendency to blow up unexpectedly during flight. This was eventually remedied by the further insulation of fuel bladders located under the engines. Another problem daunting the MiG-19 was the poor placement of its airbrakes. During deployment, severe turbulence would occur, affecting its tail plane, often producing a violent pitching up, initiating high G loads.

Engineers made an attempt to improve the reliability of the RD-9Bs. They accomplished this in part through the use of a new heat-resistant alloy, thus terminating the continual deformation to its turbine blades. Improvements in avionics culminated in the new KUS-1000 airspeed indicator, VD-20 altimeter, TP-260 backup receiver, and a gyro-flux gate compass.

All three aircraft designs, YF-100, XF4D-1, and MiG-19, were similar in some respects. They followed distinct and differentiating design philosophies to achieve the same result. The following specifications are made available to the reader in order to contrast similarities and differences that are evident in the aircraft.

	YF-100	XF4D-1	MiG-19
Wingspan (ft/in)	36' 7"	33' 6"	29' 6.5"
Length (ft/in)	46' 3"	45' 3"	42' 11.25"
Height (ft/in)	14' 5"	13'	13' 2.25"
Wing area (sq ft)	376	557	270
Weight (lb/kg) empty	18,135	16,025	12,698 (5,760)
gross	28,561	25,000	19,180 (8,700)
Engine	XJ57-P-7	XJ40-WE-8 J57-P-2	2-RD-9B
Thrust (lb/kg)			
mil	8,700 (3,946)	7,000 (3,175)	7,165 (3,250)
afterburner	13,200 (5,990)	11,600 (5,260)	14,500
Max speed	634	720	920
Service Ceiling (ft)	52,600	55,000	58,725
Rate of climb (fpm)	22,400	18,300	35,425

This photo shows how thin the F-100's inlet lip was sculpted. Note the wide stance and relatively rugged appearance of the landing gear. *Courtesy San Diego Aerospace Museum*

CHAPTER TWO

F-100 FEATURES

POWERPLANT

The heart and soul of the Super Sabre lay in its revolutionary powerplant, the legendary J57 (military) or JT3 (civilian designation) turbojet. Because of the J57's tremendous potential in both power and adaptability, it is doubtful that the Hun could have obtained and maintained its aggressive performance envelope at that time in its development.

The J57 was originally conceived by Perry W. Pratt (no relation to Francis Pratt, the cofounder of Pratt & Whitney), who at the time was head of the technical and research end of Pratt & Whitney aircraft engine company. The design drew heavily upon the company's T34 turboprop engine and the two-shaft T45. Initial J57 prototype testing was disappointing at best. In February 1949, Andy Willgoos, who was the company's chief designer, completely revamped the design by incorporating a wasp waist compressor section (area rule). The redesign provided the improvements needed for the engine to attain its legendary status.

The J57 (and civil JT3) was, in fact, probably the most significant postwar jet engine design. The engine's influence is still felt and recognized in today's jet engine designs. Not only was the J57 chosen to power the F-100 Super Sabre, it was widely used in many other military and civilian aircraft. The J57 powered just about any vehicle sprouting wings from the era—including the McDonnell F-101 Voodoo, Convair F-102 Delta Dagger, Boeing 707 airliner and B-52 Stratofortress, and Douglas DC-8, to name just a few. It also replaced, for the U.S. Navy, the disastrous Westinghouse J40 that never fully materialized in acceptable form.

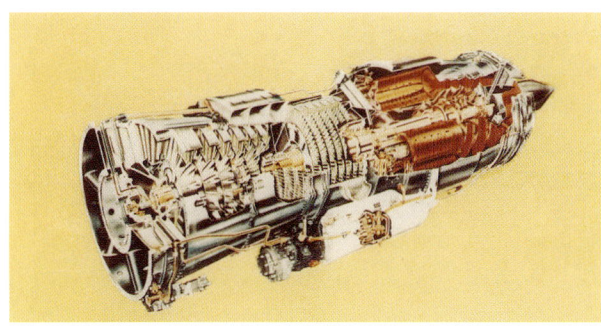

This cutaway of the Pratt & Whitney J57 or JT3 suggests the complexity of construction yet relative simplicity of operation. *Pratt & Whitney via Jack Connors*

SPECIFICATIONS
J57
Length, overall 266.92 in.
Maximum width 40.50 in.
Maximum height 47.37 in.
Compressor Axial twin spool
LP rotor 9-stage
HP rotor 7-stage
Max design pressure/ratio 12.9:1
Max primary airflow/SLS 186 lb./sec.
Combustion chamber 8-unit, can-annular
Turbine Axial 3-stage
LP rotor 2-stage
HP rotor Single-stage
Thrust max (with A/B) 19,600 lb. (J57-P-420)
14,700 lb. (J57-P-7)

A physical cutaway of the J57 (civil JT3). The panel next to the display mentions its thrust ranging from 8,700 to 13,500 pounds (19,600 pounds with afterburner), and that 21,170 were manufactured, more than any other Pratt & Whitney jet engine. *Pratt & Whitney via Jack Connors*

The J57 engine incorporated two multistage compressors—dual spool and an eight-unit cluster of can-annular combustors known as combustion chambers. It also incorporated a split three-stage turbine and the afterburner section utilizing a two-position exhaust nozzle. The two-spool compressor section consisted of a nine-stage low-pressure unit and a seven-stage high-pressure unit. Both compressor units were fully independent from each other. The first-stage turbine wheel drove the high-pressure compressor rotors and, conversely, the second- and third-stage turbines drove the low-pressure compressor rotors. When the engine was started, the lower-pressure compressor would accelerate the oncoming airflow through the nine stages and then push it into the high-pressure compressor. Incorporating the area-rule concept in the J57's design enhanced efficiency by better utilizing the airflow's kinetic energy. Of particular note, the low-pressure compressor's shaft rotated inside the high-pressure compressor shaft.

Because of both compressors' relative independence from one another, each could run at its own angular velocity, thus enhancing the airflow as well. The Westinghouse J40 and the General Electric J35 and J47 maintained the use of single compressors. The problem with this design concept was that it limited the usefulness of these engines because a single compressor assembly accommodated both low- and high-pressure compressor blades. Flow was routinely interrupted, causing flameout; compressor blades would stall; and compressor surges could result. Because thermodynamically, only certain blade pitches could be realized, this arrangement often resulted in compressor blades cracking or breaking, thus spelling the doom of the entire engine, often while in flight. These blade losses were linked to high residual stress culminating at the root of the blade during lengthy operations at high pressures and temperatures.

COMBUSTORS

The J57's eight combustors were more commonly referred to as burner cans. These combustors were of can-annular design. Fuel was sprayed into the burner can through dual-orifice nozzles situated in clusters of six located at the inlet of each combustor.

The fuel was ignited by two spark plugs located in burner cans number four and five. Upon successful ignition, the flame was carried to the other burner units by connecting flame tubes. In accordance with the Brayton cycle, a gas turbine process, the continuous combustion supplied the heat for expanding the compressed air, thus increasing the velocity of the gas flow contacting the turbine section in the completion of this cycle. The hot, expanding gases contacted all three turbines, imparting some of their momentum to rotate the blades, which, in turn, powered both of the compressors. The bulk of the mass flow escaped through the engine's nozzle and through an afterburner section attached to the nozzle if the afterburner was in use. In the case of the F-100, the afterburner assembly was paramount in achieving Mach 1 in level flight. To augment the fighter's performance, the afterburner unit was utilized to institute a temporary increase in overall engine thrust.

AFTERBURNER

The afterburner included in the J57-P-7 made up a double-wall tube. This enabled engine exhaust gases to flow through the annulus formed between the double walls, which, in turn, allowed for effective cooling of the unit.

Afterburners utilize recovery of low engine turbine exhaust gas temperature by supplementing the gas flow with the re-introduction of fuel through the fuel gutter. A flame holder, in turn, ignites this mixture of air and fuel. Drastic increases in thrust are attained instantaneously, but only for short periods due to the inordinate amounts of fuel used during afterburner operations. A two-position iris exhaust nozzle controls this re-energized flow.

INTAKE

The F-100 used a thin-lip nose air inlet designed to reduce significantly the effects of drag and increase engine duct efficiency by improving air-pressure recovery. This whole arrangement added approximately 50 knots to the F-100's maximum speed. The thin lip of the intake duct is another ambient characteristic that attributed to the fighter's high-altitude, high-speed operational performance and proved to be a distinctive trademark of the F-100's appearance. The duct design better utilized the tons of air aspirating to the plane's powerful J57 engine. Early on, it was proposed that variable ramps be built inside the F-100's fuselage to slow down the supersonic blast of air consumed through the inlet. Slowing the airflow to subsonic speeds, the fighter's J57 engine could properly ingest the air. This concept was eventually abandoned in favor of a highly modified F-86 type of fixed ramp, ram-air nose intake. The decision was considered wise from an engineering standpoint as well as a good manufacturing choice. The ram air frontal intake, embodying a rather elongated nose configuration, avoided problems associated with supersonic airflow patterns. The single duct was sufficient in length to slow supersonic air to subsonic velocities required for efficient engine operations.

FUSELAGE

The fuselage was composed of all-metal stressed skin, semi-monocoupe construction, consisting primarily of aluminum alloy with significant amounts of titanium located in the aft section of the vehicle. Titanium and its alloys solely constituted the afterburner section of the fuselage and at the time was a relatively novel material with a nasty reputation for difficulty in fabrication. The fuselage of the F-100 also had a high fineness ratio, meaning the profile of the plane's body changed shape gradually, in streamlined fashion, to keep aerodynamic drag to a minimum.

WINGS

The wings of the Super Sabre incorporated a sweep angle of 45 degrees along with its empennage (tail surfaces), utilizing a 7 percent thickness at maximum chord, and 3.5 percent for its empennage. The wing, like the fuselage, was also created with a stressed skin, semi-monocoupe construction. Each wing had split ailerons located inboard along its trailing edge. The ailerons' relative location nearer to the fuselage reduced and offset the adverse effects of wing twist and bending as the F-100 approached and exceeded Mach 1.

Positioned along the leading edge of the wing were the fighter's leading-edge slats, which enhanced the wings' lifting ability, and were referred to as high-lift devices. The slats extended and retracted automatically, depending on the aerodynamic forces acting on the wing within the F-100's flight envelope. The slats increased the maximum lift at takeoff, while delaying and limiting wing buffet in flight, thus allowing higher

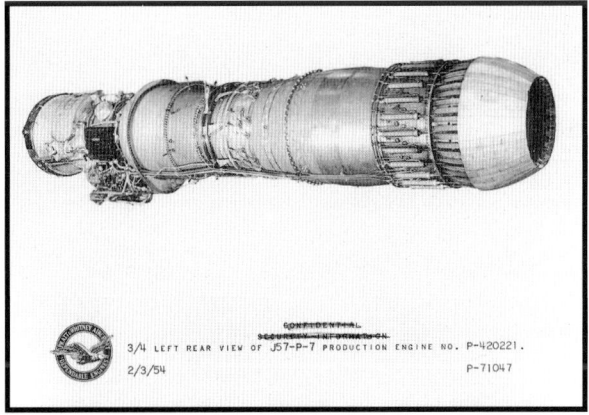

The two-position iris exhaust nozzle is visible in this three-quarter left rear view of the J57-P-7, engine no. **P-420221.** *Courtesy Pratt & Whitney via Jack Connors*

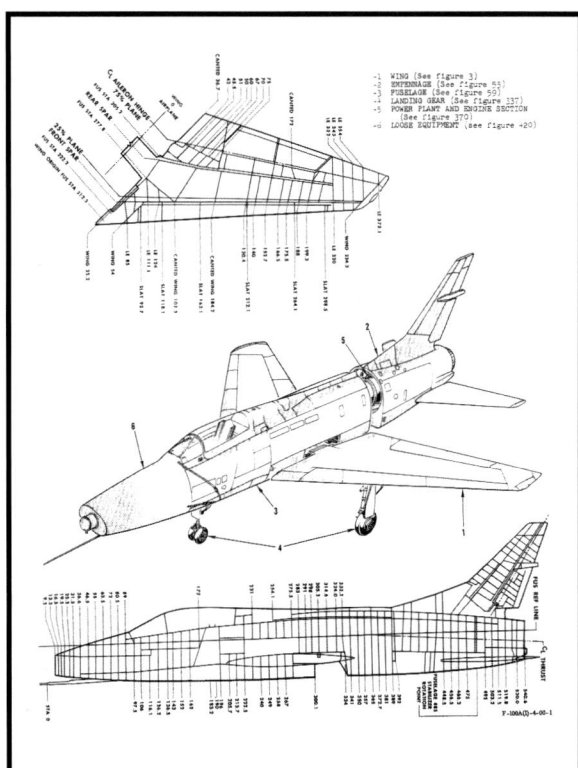

Denoted in this drawing are the fuselage and wing station assembly numbers for the F-100A. Also indicated is the rear fuselage break in order to facilitate an engine change.

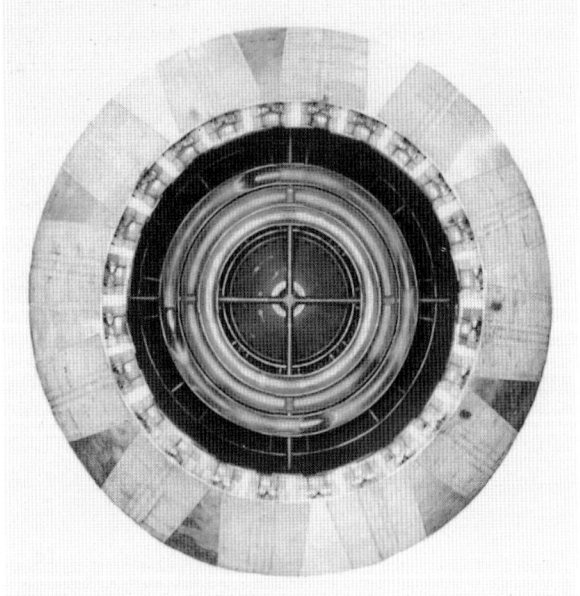

A rear shot of a J57-P-7, exposing the fuel gutter and flame holder, which are paramount in afterburner operation.

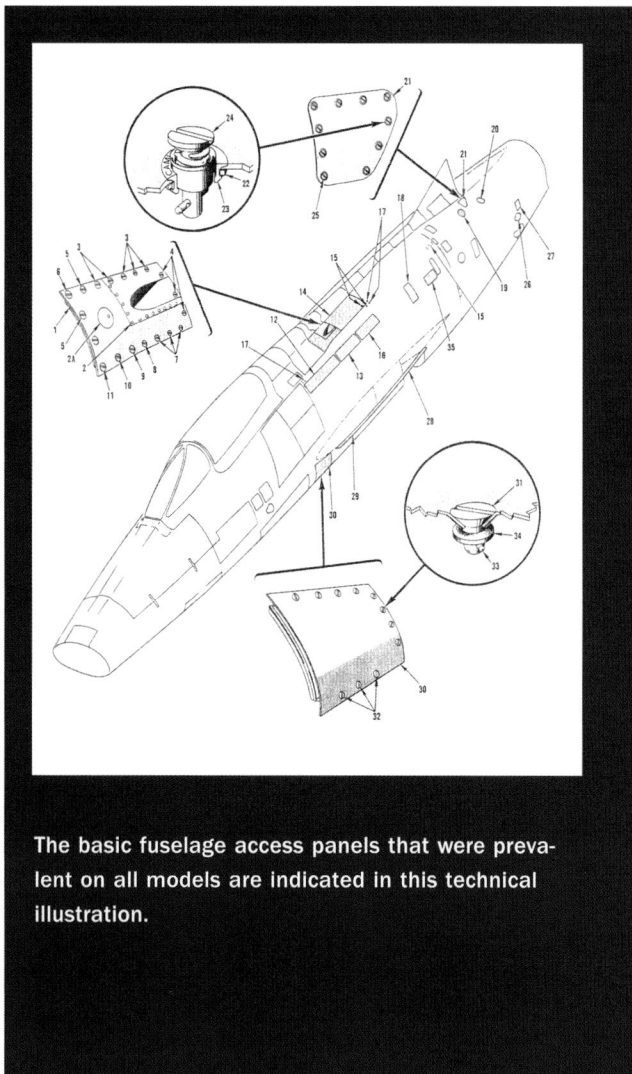

The basic fuselage access panels that were prevalent on all models are indicated in this technical illustration.

Gs to be incurred in diving turns. These high-lift devices vastly improved the lateral control characteristics of the jet near stalling speed. They also permitted tighter constant altitude turns for any given amount of engine thrust and speed.

HORIZONTAL STABILIZER

The operation and movement of the entire horizontal stabilizer maintained longitudinal control of the F-100. This arrangement, better known as a stabilator, was located and mounted below the wing chord plane positioned along the lower portion of the aft fuselage. This location placed the stabilator in a desired wing-downwash field that eliminated the pitch-up problem

FIGURE & INDEX NUMBER	PART NUMBER	1 2 3 4 5 6 7 NOMENCLATURE	UNITS PER ASSY.	USEABLE ON CODE
60 -4	192-53305-11	HEAT AND VENT SYSTEM EQUIPMENT INSTL, Canopy enclosure defroster (see fig 327 for breakdown)	NP	
-5	192-054609	ELECTRICAL EQUIP. INSTL, Canopy (see fig 265 for bkdn	NP	
-6	150-31801	ENCLOSURE INSTL, Cockpit complete (see fig 85 for bkdn	NP	
-7	192-310150-101	DOOR ASSY, Fuselage station 173 5/16 to sta 196 ammunition LH (see fig 67 for breakdown)	1	
	192-310510-102	DOOR ASSY, Fuselage station 173 5/16 to sta 196 ammunition RH (see fig 67 for breakdown)	1	
-8	192-310225	DOOR ASSY, Fuselage sta 231 to 254 1/3 upper equipment access (see fig 59 for breakdown)	1	A
	192-310225-100	DOOR ASSY, Fuselage sta 231 to 254 1/8 upper equipment access (see fig 59 for breakdown)	1	B
-9	192-310296	DOOR ASSY, Fuselage sta 214 to 231 upper access	1	
	AN509-8R9	SCREW	5	
	AN509-10R11	SCREW	13	
-10	192-31068	DOOR ASSY, Fus sta 275.5 to sta 305.375 upper deck top	1	
	AN509-10R9	SCREW	54	
-11	192-31007	TUNNEL ASSY, Fuselage sta 305 1/4 to 325 5/8	1	
	AN509-10R9	SCREW	22	
-12	192-31008	TUNNEL ASSY, Fuselage sta 325 5/8 to 341	1	
	AN509-10R9	SCREW	23	
-13	192-31009	TUNNEL ASSY, Fuselage station 341 to 365	1	
	AN509-10R8	SCREW	29	
-14	192-31010	TUNNEL ASSY, Fuselage station 365 to 389	1	
	98265-2-.220	. STUD, (United-Carr)	6	
	99836	. PIN, (United-Carr)	6	
-15	192-31025	DOOR ASSY, Fus sta 389 1/16 to 403 3/8 dorsal fin access	1	
	58265-1-.130	. STUD, (United-Carr)	12	
	58265-1-.140	. STUD, (United-Carr)	6	
	58265-2-.190	. STUD, (United-Carr)	2	
	58265-2-.200	. STUD, (United-Carr)	2	
	99836	. PIN, (United-Carr)	22	
-16	217-31042	RADOME, AT223/APG30 radar antenna, assy of (use 192-31037 or 192-31037-11 until exh)	1	
	A3235-020-24A	WASHER, (Tinnerman)	32	
	AN509-10R12	SCREW	32	
-17	192-31015-1 *2	DOOR ASSY, Fus sta 196 to 222 1/2 upper equip. access LH	1	
	192-31015-2 *2	DOOR ASSY, Fus sta 196 to 222 1/2 upper equip. access RH	1	
-18	58265-2-.210	. STUD, (United-Carr)	3	
-19	58265-4-.400	. STUD, (United-Carr)	2	
-20	99836	. PIN, (United-Carr)	14	
-21	2W1R15-19-125	. WASHER, (North American)	28	
-22	192-31016-1 *1	DOOR ASSY, Fus sta 196 to 222 1/2 lower equip. access LH	1	
	192-31016-2 *1	DOOR ASSY, Fus sta 196 to 222 1/2 lower equip. access RH	1	
	58265-2-.170	. STUD, (United-Carr)	11	
	58265-2-.210	. STUD, (United-Carr)	13	
	99836	. PIN, (United-Carr)	36	
	2W1R15-19-125	. WASHER, (North American) (see index 21)		
-23	130-310105-1	DOOR ASSY, Fus sta 125 instrument panel attaching access LH	1	
	130-310105-2	DOOR ASSY, Fus sta 125 instrument panel attaching access RH	1	
	AN509-8R8	SCREW	4	
-24	192-310211-11	DOOR, Fuselage station 143 to station 152 access LH	1	
	192-310211-12	DOOR Fuselage station 143 to station 152 access RH	1	
	AN509-10R8	SCREW	25	
-25	192-31017-11	DOOR, Fuselage station 152 to fuselage station 162 access LH	1	
	192-31017-12	DOOR, Fuselage station 152 to fuselage station 162 access RH	1	
	AN509-10R10	SCREW	40	
-26	192-31049-1	DOOR ASSY, Fus sta 222 1/2 to 231 heat and vent access LH	1	
	192-31049-2	DOOR ASSY, Fus sta 222 1/2 to 231 heat and vent access RH	1	
	58265-1-.110	. STUD, (United-Carr)	5	
	58265-3-.250	. STUD, (United-Carr)	2	
	99836	. PIN, (United-Carr)	7	
-27	192-310293	DOOR ASSY, Fus canted sta 211.938 upper access	1	C
	192-312330	. SEAL ASSY, Fus canted sta 211.938 upper	1	C
	SP1561-1032-10	SCREW, (Shakeproof)	6	C
-28	235-530078-3	DECAL, Warning markings, exterior fuselage	2	
-29	235-530078-5	DECAL, Warning markings, fuselage	2	

*1 192-31015-1 and -2 hand fitted on airplanes 26-134. Use 192-319016-1 or -2 for spares.
*2 192-31015-1 and -2 hand fitted on airplanes 26-134. Use 192-319015-1 or -2 for spares.

USEABLE ON CODE: A 53-1531 thru 53-1629
B 53-1637 and subs
C 53-1550 and subs

encountered by aircraft incorporating a high-positioned stabilizer. This condition was prevalent during turns and pull-ups encountered at transonic and supersonic speeds. The F-100 was the first USAF aircraft to employ this design innovation.

FLAPS AND SPEED BRAKES

Wing flaps were not part of the design for the A and C versions of the Super Sabre. They were later introduced on the D and F variants. Primary speed reduction was achieved through the extension of a hydraulically operated, electrically controlled speed brake located on the underside of the fuselage positioned forward of the main landing gear wheelwell. This speed brake was frequently used for auxiliary speed control in all flight conditions, and, in combat, the brake enhanced and permitted tighter turning maneuvers. It was of particular note that the speed brake could be employed at any speed with only a minimum amount of pitch changes occurring. Provisions were designed into the plane's systems so that in the event of hydraulic failure, the speed brake could be retracted to a trailing position with a mechanically controlled dump valve.

HYDRAULIC POWER SYSTEM

The Super Sabre possessed three separate, constant-pressure-type hydraulic systems. The first was the utility hydraulic system, while the other two were referred to as the flight-control hydraulic system. The latter were further identified by flight-control systems one and two. Engine-driven 3,000-psi hydraulic pumps independently pressurized the utility system and the dual flight-control systems. The J57's forward accessory section drove both the utility hydraulic pump and the pump for flight-control system number one as well.

The pump that operated flight control system number two was powered by the main accessory drive located at the lower front end of the engine. There was also auxiliary power derived from a ram-air turbine, which would pressurize flight control system number one in the event of an emergency. This, in turn, drove a constant-displacement hydraulic pump.

UTILITY HYDRAULIC SYSTEM

The utility hydraulic system comprised a 3,000-psi pressure-type closed center system. The system supplied pressure to the following units: the landing gear and its doors, wheel brakes, speed brake, nose-wheel steering, the gun and ammunition compartment purge doors, the yaw damper system, ram-air turbine doors, and, finally, the horizontal stabilizer trim impulse system. The fluid used to operate and maintain the utility hydraulic system was housed in a 2.69-gallon reservoir, which was augmented by a variable-volume engine-driven pump.

FLIGHT-CONTROL HYDRAULIC SYSTEMS

The two complete but independent hydraulic systems operating simultaneously during the operation of the Hun's flight controls (better known as the number one and number two systems) were responsible for the proper operation of the ailerons and the one-piece, all-moving horizontal stabilizer. Each system was designed to be fed by separate engine-driven pumps. In the event of the failure of one system, the other system would assume the entire workload, but at half the original power. In the event of a total engine failure, or if both systems failed, power was then restored by the use of the ram-air-turbine emergency pump.

The control-surface hydraulic-control valves were positioned mechanically by the deflection of the control stick or displacement of the rudder pedals. These valves then directed the flow of hydraulic fluid to the actuating cylinders in order to move the control surfaces. Of special note, the dual control valves and the tandem type of actuating cylinders worked independently from one another. When movement of control surfaces occurred, a follow-up mechanism immediately returned the control valve to its neutral position, thus disabling hydraulic flow to the hydraulic cylinder, thus shutting it off. Irreversibility was maintained by means of check valves.

This is how both sides of the all-moving horizontal stabilizer are fastened together. Note its sheer simplicity.

COCKPIT

The cockpit in the F-100 was the nerve center where

FIGURE & INDEX NUMBER	PART NUMBER	1 2 3 4 5 6 7 NOMENCLATURE	UNITS PER ASSY.	USEABLE ON CODE
53	217-23001	*1 STABILIZER ASSY, Vertical (complete) (use 192-23501 or -51 untl. exh) (see figure 51 for next assembly)	Ref	
	192-23811-51	. TIP ASSEMBLY, Vertical stabilizer (mod) (use 192-23811 untl. exh)	1	
-1	192-230812	. . CAP, Vertical stabilizer tip.	1	
-1A	192-230803	. . LEADING EDGE, Vertical stabilizer, aluminum tip.	1	
-1B	192-23820	. . BEAM, Vertical stabilizer tip trailing edge.	1	
-2	192-23345	. . WASHER, Plastic flush rivet.	60	
	192-054608	. ELECTRICAL EQUIPMENT INSTALLATION, Vertical stabilizer. . . .	NP	
-3	AN515-8R10	. . SCREW.	2	
-4	192-54160	. . GASKET, Electrical vertical stabilizer light assembly. . .	1	
	S1123	. . LIGHT ASSEMBLY, Two unit tail (Soderberg) (use S1023B untl exh) (RDI DS566)	1	
-5	AN3124-307	. . LAMP (RDI 1536)	2	
-6	192-23348-1	. FAIRING, Vertical stabilizer LH	1	
	217-23002	. FRAME ASSEMBLY, Vertical stabilizer	1	
-7	217-23347-1	. . FAIRING ASSEMBLY, Vertical stabilizer vent tube. . . . . . forward LH	1	
-8	217-23348	. . FAIRING, Vertical stabilizer vent tube RH (use 217-23347-2 with 192-23348-2 untl exh)	1	
-9	AN509-416R18	. . SCREW, (on LH side).	1	
	AN509-416R16	. . SCREW, (on RH side).	1	
-10	2W18-416	. . WASHER, (North American)	2	
-11	AN364-428	. . NUT.	2	
-12	AN509-10R11	. . SCREW.	4	
-13	2W18-10	. . WASHER, (North American)	4	
-14	AN365-1032	. . NUT.	4	
-15	217-23410	. . FITTING ASSEMBLY, Vertical stabilizer station 77.312 . . . hinge (whn exh use 217-23428-5)	1	
	217-23428-5	. . FITTING ASSEMBLY, Vertical stabilizer station 77.312 . . . hinge (use 217-23410 untl exh)	1	
-16	192-23351	. . . RETAINER, Vertical stabilizer station 77.312 hinge. . . bearing	1	
-17	AN200KS5	. . . BEARING.	1	
-18	217-23410-3	. . . FITTING, Vertical stabilizer station 77.312 hinge . . .	1	
	217-23428-3	. . . FITTING, Vertical stabilizer station 77.312 hinge . . .	1	
-19	217-23427-3	. . FITTING, Vertical stabilizer station 30.95 hinge . . . . . (use 217-23409 untl exh)	1	
-20	217-23408-3	. . FITTING ASSEMBLY, Vertical stabilizer rear beam . . . . . root attaching	1	
	4B19M-S7-018	. . BUSHING, (North American)	1	
-21	192-23407	. . FITTING, Vertical stabilizer front beam root attaching . .	1	
-22	217-23412	. . FITTING, Vertical stabilizer rear beam vent tube . . . . . doubler RH	1	
-23	192-48072	. TUBE ASSY, Fuel vent outlet complete	1	
-24	192-54401	. CONDUIT, Electrical tail light.	1	
-25	192-23805	. DOOR ASSY, Vertical stabilizer plastic tip.	1	
		ATTACHING PARTS		
-26	AN509-10R12	. SCREW	43	
-27	AN509-8R9	. SCREW	12	
		---*---		
-28	192-23381	. CONDUIT, Vertical stabilizer antenna cable.	1	
-29	217-71008	. RADIO EQUIPMENT INSTALLATION, Vertical stabilizer . . . . . section (see fig. 296 for bkdn)	NP	
-30	280	. DISCHARGER ASSY, Electrostatic (Gayston)(use 243-71231-11 . . untl exh)	1	
		ATTACHING PARTS		
-31	AN364-832	. NUT	2	
-32	2W18-8L	. WASHER, (North American).	2	
-33	NAS220-8	. SCREW	2	
		---*---		

*1 When ordering a spare stabilizer assembly specify part number 235-230901-301.

the pilot operated all electromechanical and hydraulic controls necessary to insure the proper operation of the aircraft.

FLIGHT CONTROLS: All essential control surfaces were operated by control stick and rudder pedal controls initiated through an irreversible hydraulic control system. Each aileron assembly consisted of an inboard and an outboard panel that were actuated as one unit. This allowed unimpaired lateral control, which resulted from in-flight wing deflections. The horizontal stabilizer, or stabilator, was a one-piece unit. The rudder was of splitter design, which allowed for airflow separation off the trailing edge to reduce significantly rudder flut-

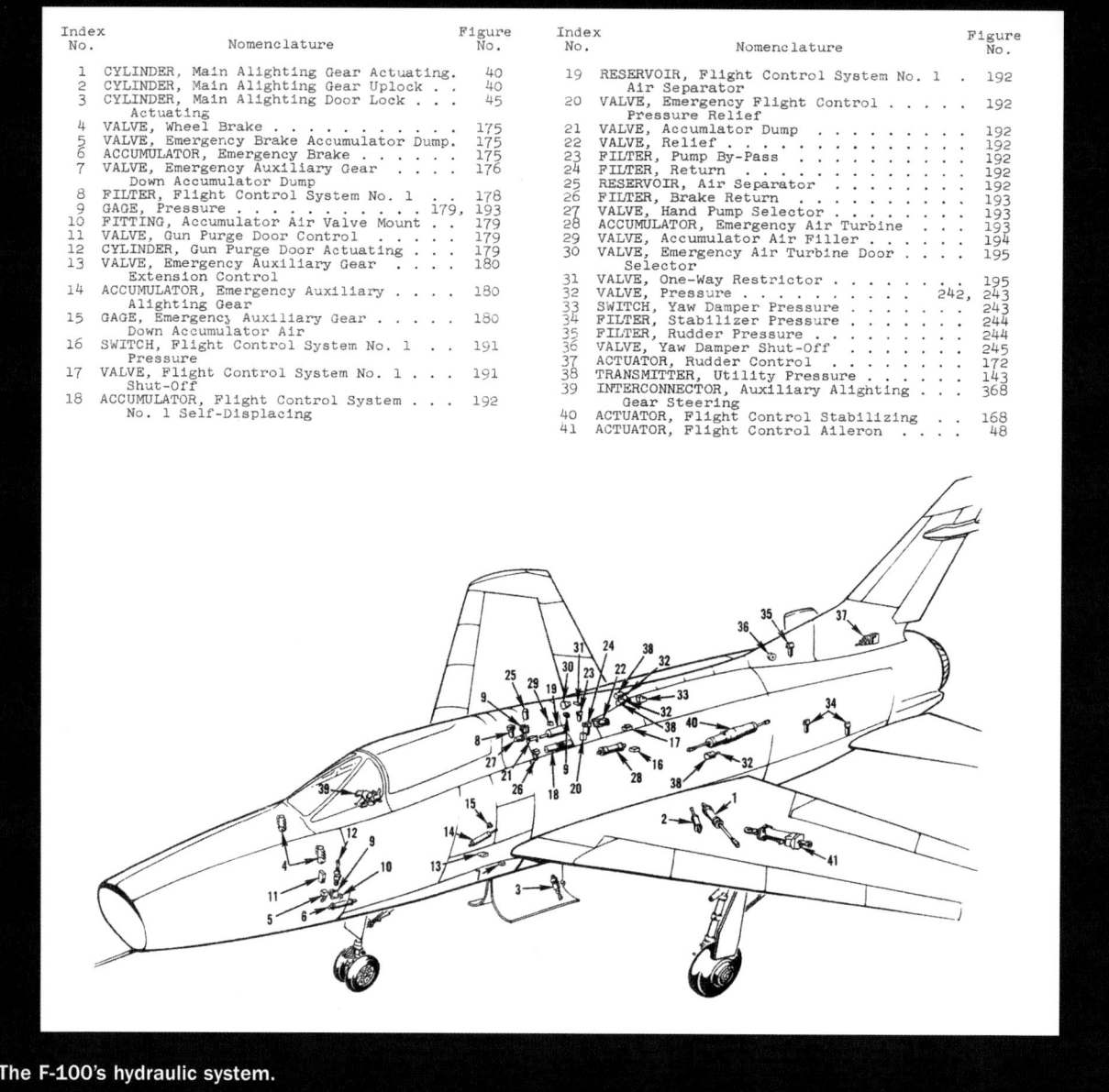

The F-100's hydraulic system.

ter. The rudder's fabrication was split chord-wise in two sections joined by a hinge. This was necessary to offset any rudder binding because of any deflection incurred by the entire vertical stabilizer. A dampener to reduce and eliminate any vibration experienced through any incidental rudder flutter occurring at high speeds also accompanied the rudder.

The irreversible nature of the F-100's hydraulic systems held the control surfaces against any forces that did not stem from control movements and prevented the forces in question from being transmitted back to the controls. Therefore, the pilot did not feel the aerodynamic loads experienced by the control surfaces. Because of this condition, an artificial feel system was built into the controls so the pilot would not overfly the aircraft resulting in the destruction of the fighter and perhaps the ultimate death of the flyer. This system also accounted for trimming the aircraft in flight, therefore negating the need for any kind of trim tabs.

The control yoke or stick was mechanically fastened to hydraulic control valves located at the aileron and horizontal stabilizer hydraulic actuators. Movement of the stick positioned these control valves so that power from the movement of these valves was transferred to the control surface, actuating movement to the control surfaces. When the desired control surface deflection was obtained, a follow-up system automatically shut off the hydraulic fluid to the actuators. Located on the control stick were a host of devices to aid and sustain control over the Hun. The lateral and longitudinal trim switch, as well as the nose-wheel steering button, gun trigger, radar reject switch, and bomb "pickle" button completed the stick's various controls.

RUDDER PEDALS: The rudder pedals were of the hanger type, which were mechanically connected to a hydraulic control valve located at the rudder. Rudder deflection was initiated during the event of pedal movement. During movement, the control valve was positioned to route power from the utility hydraulic system to the rudder-actuating cylinder. Upon reaching the desired rudder position, a follow-up system then terminated the hydraulic flow to the actuating cylinder. In the event of a utility hydraulic system failure, a mechanical linkage from the pedals achieved effective rudder control. Primary braking and thus, ground steering, was also achieved through use of the rudder pedals.

COCKPIT ENVIRONMENTAL CONTROL: The cockpit environmental control system furnished air conditioned, heated, and pressurized air for the cockpit environment. Air needed for the successful operation of the system was extracted from the engine compressor and was passed through a primary heat exchanger into the refrigeration unit. The cooled air and the heated air were mixed to obtain the desired cockpit temperature set by the pilot. A pressurization control unit maintained a constant pressure differential of 2.75 psi. This occurred between altitudes of 21,200 to 31,000 feet. A constant pressure differential of 5 psi was maintained above 31,000 feet in altitude. Bleed air from the engine's compressor was also taken from the primary heat exchanger and circulated around the canopy and front windshield to defrost and prevent the formation of ice or fogging often experienced during high-speed dives.

CONTROL PANEL INSTRUMENTS: Most of the control panel instruments were powered by the aircraft's electrical system, while the exhaust temperature gauge and tachometer systems were of the self-generating type.

ENGINE CONTROL THROTTLE: The throttle was mechanically linked to the fuel-control unit for regulating the engine power output, controlling various engine and fuel systems. When the engine's master switch was actuated and the throttle lever advanced beyond the off position, the electrically driven fuel booster pumps and the fuel transfer pump located in the intermediate tank were engaged. If the starter and ignition button were pressed, along with the throttle advancement, this initialized the engine ignition circuit. Additional forward displacement of the throttle to the idle position completely opened the fuel cutoff valve, thus initiating automatic fuel flow to the engine in accordance to throttle setting.

However, on the two-place F-100F variant, there were two throttle quadrants, the first located in the forward cockpit and the second located in the rear cockpit tub. Cables interconnected the throttles, and any movement or position initiated by one throttle was duplicated in displacement by the second. On a special note, each throttle lever was autonomous from one another in outboard/inboard travel. A retractable solenoid-operator

An inside shot of a typical F-100A cockpit enclosure.
Courtesy Jay Miller Aviation History Collection

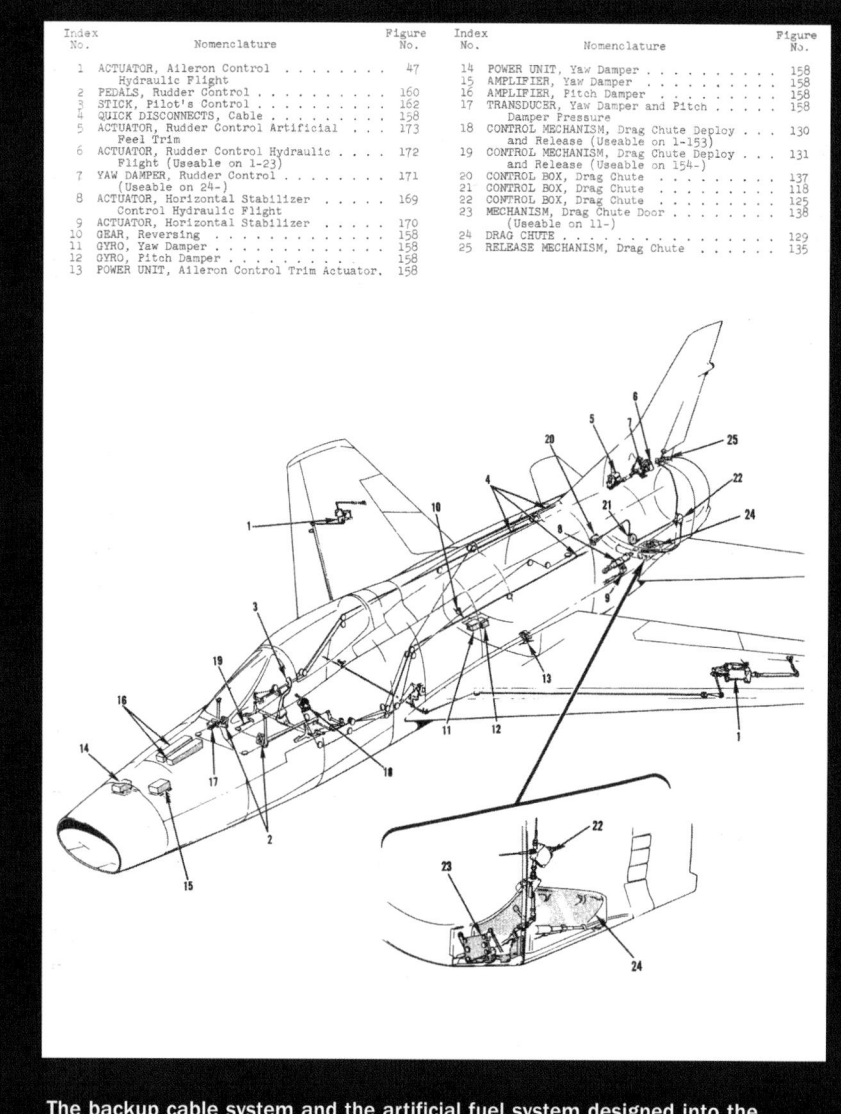

The backup cable system and the artificial fuel system designed into the flight-control system so the pilot wouldn't overfly the aircraft.

idle stop prevented the rear operation of the throttle through any inadvertent movement to the off position.

AFTERBURNER CONTROL: To obtain afterburner actuation, the pilot advanced the throttle outbound in the forward part of the throttle quadrant from military to the afterburner setting. Upon selection, the tank-mounted afterburner fuel booster pump was energized and the afterburner system was activated. There was an override spring incorporated in the throttle's design that prevented any inadvertent movements to the afterburner setting. A force of 9 pounds was required to move the throttle to afterburner selection and about 18 pounds of force were required for its disengagement.

EJECTION SEAT: The pilot's ejection seat was probably the most important safety feature offered in the Super Sabre's design. The pilot, sitting upright in the seat, in the event of a catastrophe could escape from the stricken craft without incident. The ejection seat permitted ejection at any speed or altitude during flight. There were two types of seats offered in the Hun. Power for the first type of seat centered on an explosive cartridge. Actuated during an emergency, the concentrated blast supplied the necessary force to expel both pilot and seat quickly from the aircraft. The second type of ejection seat featured in the F-100 was powered by both a cartridge and rocket, which developed 7,500 pounds of thrust, thus enhancing low-altitude ejection capabilities. The ballistic rocket–powered ejection seat also featured a quick disconnect to disable the seat during an emergency rescue.

CANOPY: The canopy was designed and fabricated as a one-piece, clamshell-type employing the use of an electromechanical mechanism for normal operation. In the event of an emergency, a cartridge-type device was used to jettison the canopy. Hinges at the rear enabled the canopy to be raised or lowered through a 22-degree arch. A switch located in the cockpit on the control panel controlled the normal operation of the canopy. External switches located on both sides of the cockpit could also be utilized in the normal operation of the canopy as well. During emergency operation, the canopy could be jettisoned either by the ejection seat handgrips being raised or through the independent use of a jettison lever located in the cockpit. Provisions were also made for the mechanical release of the canopy executed from within the cockpit or externally. Pressurization of the cockpit was initialized through the canopy seal located around the periphery or rim of the canopy as it contacted the aircraft structure upon closure.

RADIO AND RADAR: Communication for the Super Sabre was provided via the AN/ARC-34 command radio equipment providing the pilot with a frequency range from 225.0 to 399.9 megacycles. The radio control panel installation gave the pilot a selection of twenty preset channels, or, if desired, the operating frequencies could be selected manually without disruption of original preset frequencies. Two receivers were included in this equipment. The main receiver facilitated all normal reception functions. The second receiver (the guard receiver) was ground-tuned to a guard frequency and could not be altered without complete removal from the aircraft. When a new frequency was chosen, an automatic tuning mechanism altered the transmitter and receiver to accommodate that new frequency. The entire tuning cycle required around four seconds to achieve. Some of the F-100's command radio was powered by the secondary bus and on other aircraft the primary bus. The electrical system for the F-100 incorporated both direct and alternating current arrangements. The Hun also utilized an AN/ARN-6 radio compass, an AN/APX-6 identification radar, and an AN/APG-30 gun-ranging radar housed in a truncated area above the frontal portion of the intake duct.

LANDING GEAR: The F-100 had a tricycle landing gear arrangement, all of which was of air-oil oleo-struts design for shock absorption during landing. High-pressure pneumatic tires were attached to segmented rotor-type disc brakes mounted on the axles at the bottom of the struts. Dual wheels were incorporated on the F-100's nose strut. The retractable tricycle landing gear was electrically controlled and hydraulically actuated. The main gear strut assemblies retracted inward, and were covered by the underside wheelwell doors. The dual-wheel front assembly retracted aft into the forward fuselage underside. An electrically activated retractable tailskid operated in unison with the landing gear.

The F-100 was also equipped with a tail-arresting hook that was only employed to stop the Hun during takeoff and landing emergencies. It was locked externally in the aft portion of the aircraft just ahead of the tailskid. It was held in the loaded position and actuated by a solenoid latch. Upon activation, the spring-steel hook was held against the runway by spring tension.

Provisions were also incorporated in the actuation of the landing gear during a hydraulic or electrical failure. In both modes, emergency or normal, the average gear-lowering time ranged between six to eight seconds. Also of particular note, a load switch located on each main gear shock strut prevented premature retraction while the aircraft lay static on the ground. However, an override switch was also incorporated for gear retraction in this mode.

ELECTRICAL POWER SUPPLY SYSTEM: The F-100 utilized a 28-volt AC power system powered by an engine-driven generator. Accompanying this system was a 24-volt, 24-ampere-hour battery standby power source. The AC power was provided by a single-phase inverter and either of two three-phase inverters. When the aircraft was idle on the ground, DC power was then supplied from external sources.

FUEL SYSTEM: Synonymous to all F-100 variants were the fuel tanks located in the fuselage. The C, D, and F variants incorporated fuel cells in the wings. All models A thru F incorporated wing drop tanks to augment fuel capacity. Models C, D, and F also were equipped with an in-flight refueling capacity.

The fuselage fuel system embodied in all models supplied fuel to the thirsty J57 engine. Standard arrangement called for three fuselage fuel tanks, which were, in turn, managed sequentially and automatically by either gravity feed or electrical fuel transfer pumps. This was accomplished in order to maintain the Hun's center of gravity limits needed to sustain normal flight characteristics. All fuel traveling to the engine passed through what was called an inverted flight tank positioned in the right cell of the fuselage intermediate tank. This tank retained about 1.6 gallons of jet fuel, which was used when the aircraft was pulling negative Gs for brief periods only. The maximum fuel capacity of each model F-100 was one of the basic defining factors that differentiated one model from the other.

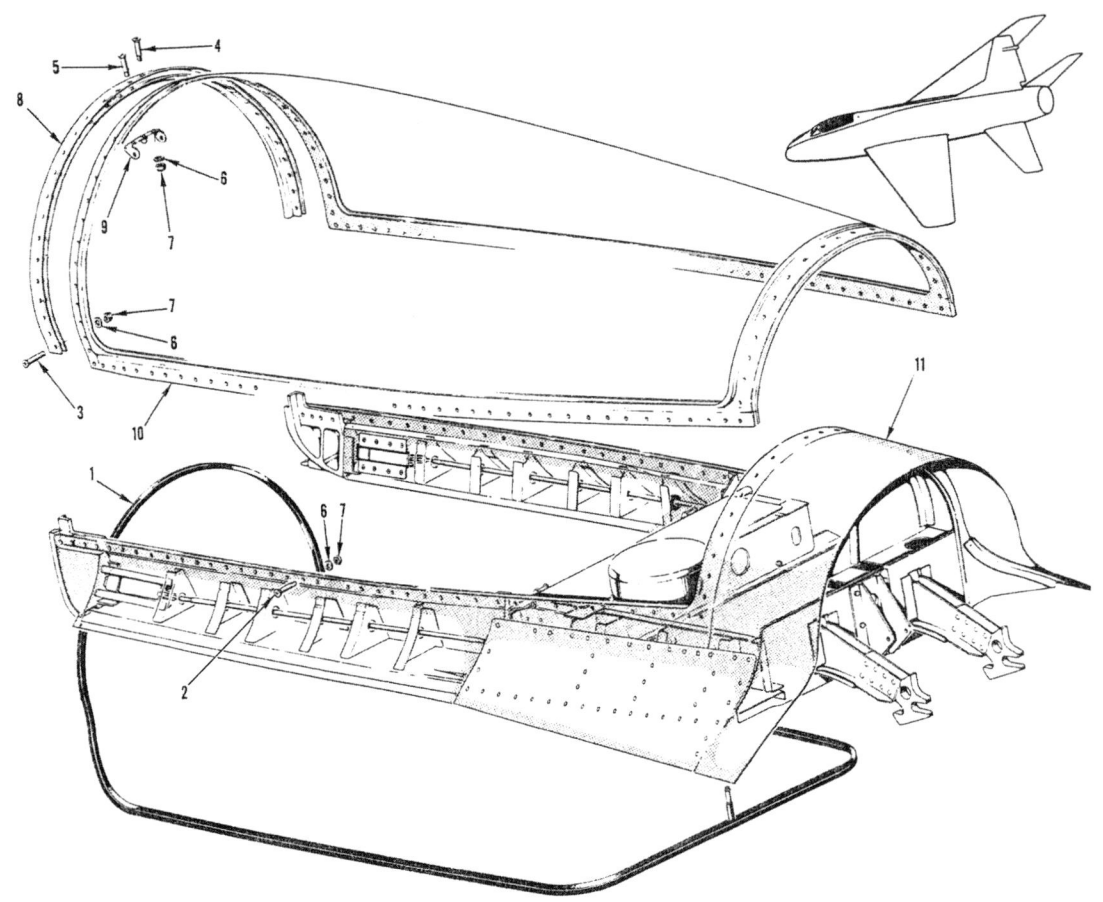

FIGURE & INDEX NUMBER	PART NUMBER	1 2 3 4 5 6 7 NOMENCLATURE	UNITS PER ASSY.	USEABLE ON CODE
90	180-31802-21	CANOPY ASSY, Cockpit enclosure (use 180-31802 or 180-31802-11 untl exh) (see fig. 85 for next assy)	Ref	
	180-31802-11	CANOPY ASSY, Cockpit enclosure (use 180-31802 untl exh) (whn exh use 180-31802-21) (see fig. 85 for next assembly)	Ref	
	180-31802	CANOPY ASSY, Cockpit enclosure (whn exh 180-31802-11 or 180-31802-21) (see figure 85 for next assembly)	Ref	
-1	180-31825	. SEAL ASSEMBLY, Cockpit enclosure canopy inflatable	1	
-2	AN509-10R14	. SCREW	65	
-3	AN509-10R17	. SCREW	26	
-4	AN509-10R18	. SCREW	4	
	AN509-10R16	. SCREW	25	
	AN509-10R19	. SCREW	10	
-5	AN509-416R19	. SCREW	1	
-6	AN960D10L	. WASHER	130	
-7	AN364-1032	. NUT	130	
-8	180-31804-11	. BOW, Cockpit encl canopy (on 180-31802-21 & -11 only)	1	
	180-31804	. BOW, Cockpit enclosure canopy (on 180-31802 only)	1	
-9	180-53076-11	. BRACKET, Rear view mirror support	1	
-10	180-31803	. GLASS ASSEMBLY, Cockpit enclosure canopy	1	
-11	180-31837-201 *2	. FRAME ASSY, Cockpit enclosure canopy complete (whn exh use 180-31837-111) (see fig. 92 for breakdown)	1	
	180-31837-111 *2	. FRAME ASSY, Cockpit enclosure canopy complete (see fig. 92 for breakdown) (use 180-31837-201 untl exh)	1	
	180-31837-101 *1	. FRAME ASSY, Cockpit encl canopy complete (use 180-31837 untl exh) (see fig. 92 for breakdown)	1	
	180-31837 *1	. FRAME ASSY, Cockpit encl canopy complete (whn exh use 180-31837-101) (see fig. 92 for breakdown)	1	

*1 Used on 180-31802 canopy only.
*2 Used on 180-31802-11 and 180-31802-21 only.

The clamshell canopy was molded out of Plexiglas and maintained its integrity under extreme conditions as well as supersonic speeds.

Index No.	Nomenclature	Figure No.
1	SUPPORT, Tank Sway Brace Retractable	32
2	MECHANISM, Tank Support Release	37
3	TANK, Underwing Drop Tank	33
4	VALVE, Air Pressure Relief and Drain	38
5	VALVE, Swing Check	38
6	SWITCH, Fuel Tank Jettison	276
7	SWITCH, Fuel Regulator	279
8	VALVE, Drop Tank Air Shut-Off	392
9	TANK UNIT	144, 147
10	PUMP, Booster	394, 401
11	VALVE, Drop Tank Level Control	411
12	VALVE, Intermediate Cell Transfer Line Shut-Off	412
13	VALVE, Forward Dive Vent	395
14	VALVE, Forward Climb Vent	395
15	CELL, Forward	395
16	MANIFOLD, Sump	399
17	CELL, Forward Lower	398
18	VALVE, Intermediate Dive Vent	400
19	VALVE, Intermediate Climb Vent	400
20	TANK, Inverted Flight	408
21	ADAPTER, Engine Feed	409
22	CELL, Intermediate	406
23	VALVE, Gravity Outlet	414
24	VALVE, Booster Pump Outlet	414
25	CELL, Aft	413
26	VALVE, Relief	410
27	SWITCH, Pressure	417
28	GAGE, Pressure	416
29	REDUCER, Pneumatic Pressure	416
30	CYLINDER, Nitrogen	416
31	VALVE, Shut-Off	416
32	TUBE, Vent Outlet	52
33	HANDLE, Wing Tank Emergency Release Cockpit	419

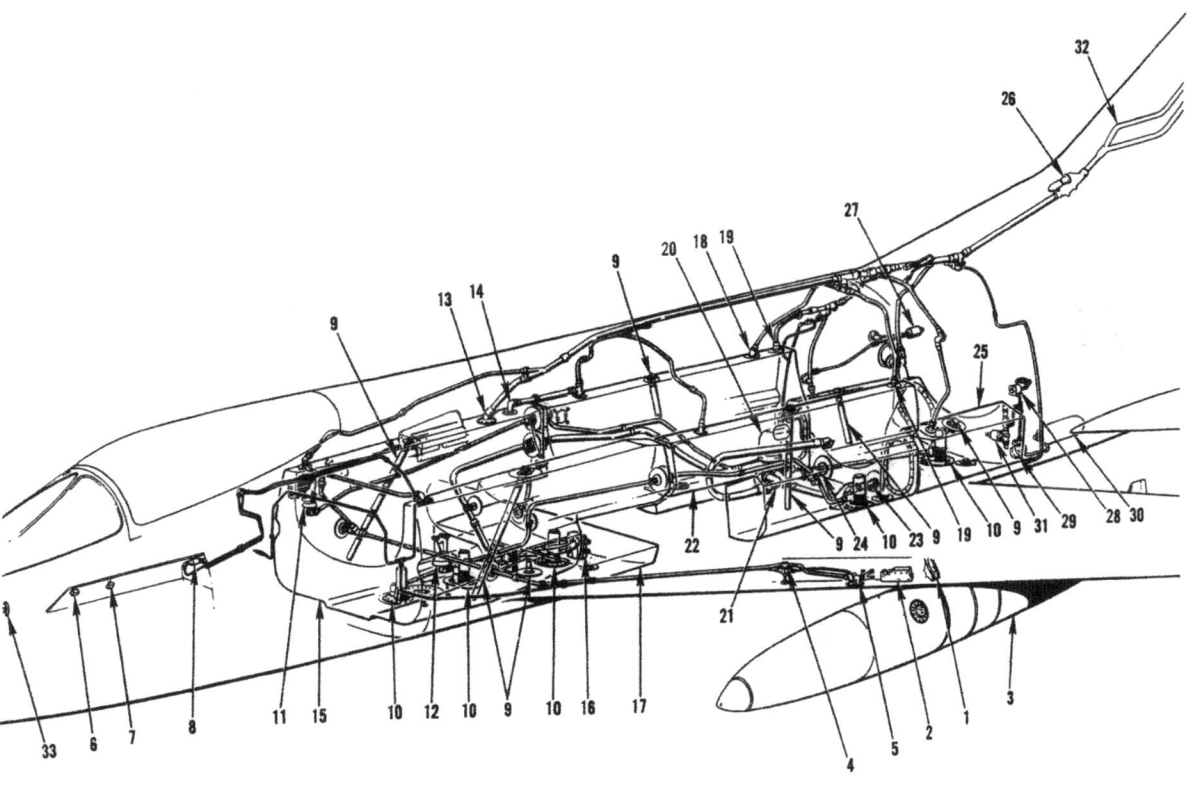

This was the basic fuselage fuel system utilized in all examples. Fuel delivery changed slightly with the advent of the wet-wing fuel cell additions incorporated on the C, D, and F models.

F-100C Super Sabre s/n 54-2099 on a routine check flight. *Courtesy David W. Menard*

CHAPTER THREE
FLIGHT TEST

THE FIRST YF-100A was completed on schedule, 24 April 1953, and arrangements were made to begin its test flight program at North American's flight test operations facility at the North Base of the Air Force's Flight Test Center (AFFTC). This was located at Edwards Air Force Base, situated in the Mojave Desert one hundred miles northeast of North American's Los Angeles aircraft production plant.

On 25 May 1953, the Super Sabre was saddled and bridled, ready for North American Chief Test Pilot George S. Welch to put her through her paces. Welch, at that time, was a rather celebrated figure, an icon for fellow pilots to revere. On 7 December 1941, during the sneak attack on Pearl Harbor, Welch, along with four other army aviators, were able to become airborne and engage the enemy. Welch scored four aerial victories during the ensuing Japanese onslaught.

Joining Welch on this historic test fight was Lieutenant Colonel Frank K. (Pete) Everest, Jr., who at that time was chief of AFFTC's flight test operations laboratory. He would accompany Welch in the cockpit of an F-86 Sabre, flying chase to the YF-100A on its maiden flight.

Everest became airborne first, circling to position himself for Welch's soon anticipated takeoff. As he closed on Welch's wing from behind, Welch pushed the Super

George Welch, chief NAA test pilot, getting ready to climb aboard YF-100 shipment no. 1. *North American Aviation via David W. Menard*

Sabre into full afterburner and soon joined Everest above the high desert over Rogers Dry Lake. The duo quickly climbed to 20,000 feet and leveled off for a quick system check on the Hun. Upon attaining 35,000 feet, Welch lit the afterburner once again and effortlessly slipped the bonds of transonic flight to exceed Mach 1.

That first fight lasted 57 minutes, accompanied by a second fight performed later that day lasting only 20 minutes. Upon confirmation of the flights, the PR types at North American Aviation were ecstatic, cheerfully boasting that the Super Sabre was the world's first operational supersonic jet fighter. Six more flights were successfully attempted that month, two of which were flown on 27 May and the remaining four on 29 May.

Rudder flutter was encountered on the eighth and ninth flights but was quickly rectified by the addition of hydraulic rudder dampers. As the test flight program proceeded, USAF officers, located at both the Wright Air Development Center (WADC) and AFFTC facilities had reservations and developing suspicions regarding to the YF-100A's actual performance. The air force embraced a more conservative approach to the test program, which came into direct conflict with NAA's more aggressive posture.

In spite of misgivings within the U.S. Air Force, the YF-100A was achieving and sustaining spectacular performance margins and as of 5 July 1953, the plane had participated in high-speed dives from 30,000 feet at speeds up to and including Mach 1.4. In spite of George Welch's preferential treatment as primary test pilot for Phase I flights, NAA pilots Daniel Darnell and Joseph Lynch also flew the prototype. Combined, they logged forty-three fights.

Phase II of the fight test program began unofficially on 11 August 1953, and was staffed with WADC Commander Colonel William F. Barnes, Richard Johnson, and "Pete" Everest in the air force fight evaluation of the YF-100A prototype. It was stipulated that Phase II begin as soon as possible and be terminated no later than May of 1954. In actuality, Phase II was initiated on 3 September 1953, required some thirty-nine fights, and was terminated on 17 September with a total accumulated flight time of nineteen hours and forty-two minutes involving the first YF-100A (s/n 52-5754).

Lieutenant Colonel Frank K. (Pete) Everest, Jr. set a speed record in YF-100 shipment no. 1. *USAF via David W. Menard*

Unknown USAF pilot about to depart the North American Aviation factory in his brand-new F-100A. *Courtesy David W. Menard*

The USAF test pilots who flew the Hun testified to the fact that it outperformed any other production fighter then in the air force's inventory. They speculated that the fighter had vast potential as a useful weapons system. They did cite several deficiencies hampering the Hun's eventual acceptance operationally. Three major reasons listed were: (1) poor visibility over the nose during takeoff and landing, (2) neutral and negative static longitudinal stability in high-speed level flight, and (3) poor low-speed handling characteristics.

Air force pilots reported that lateral and directional damping was unsatisfactory at all flight conditions and altitudes. Without the use of flaps, landings in the Super Sabre were fast and dangerous, especially at night. The plane demonstrated an uncontrollable yaw and pitching motion near its stalling speed. It was also noted that the YF-100A was not a good gun platform.

"Pete" Everest, especially, was not happy with the Hun and expressed his concerns in his official assessment of the YF-100A's flying qualities. This young but experienced USAF test pilot team had found many problems with the fledgling Hun. When NAA officials became aware of these cited shortcomings, they responded with defiance and disdain.

Some senior U.S. Air Force officials maintained the same posture as that taken by NAA officials and authorized the acceleration of the F-100's development. This catastrophic decision would soon be the center of strident controversy, eventually to the regret of all involved.

At North American's factory, the first production F-100A was completed on 25 September 1953, three weeks ahead of schedule. By October of 1953, the two YF-100As and a production F-100A were flying. As 1953 passed into 1954, production of the F-100A was well underway. Provisions were made by the air force to convert the last 70 of the F-100As to F-100Cs for the sole purpose of delivering tactical nuclear weapons.

Tactical Air Command (TAC) accepted its first Hun on 18 September 1954. Soon after, frontline air force pilots were also experiencing stability and control problems. Many pilots felt the vertical stabilizer was not large enough, and there was much debate with NAA engineers over its true dimensions. Many NAA engineers were concerned about horizontal stabilizer flutter. In fact, more effort was afforded in perfecting the 3.5 percent thickness/chord (t/c) ratio than the vertical stabilizer.

Great effort was afforded to the horizontal stabilizer because NAA engineers predicted that the dreaded flutter would occur sooner, as much as 90 knots lower, on the 3.5 percent t/c ratio unit than the 7 percent t/c stabilizer. They tested the new surface to great lengths on a rocket sled up to speeds of Mach 1.22. After many failures, modifications to the aircraft's hydraulics, including hydraulically damping the stabilator, were successfully made, and final approval was given for the stabilizer to be incorporated in production F-100As. As a point in fact, the longitudinal stability problem encountered, especially in the first production F-100As, was aggravated by a decision rendering the F-100A production aircraft with a significantly smaller vertical stabilizer than was built into both YF-100As. Company test pilot Joseph Lynch, after his first flight in an F-100A production example, quite candidly remarked on its inherent and chronic instability. At the beckoning of the chosen few who gave firsthand explanations of the aberrant handling characteristics of the aircraft, some changes were made. In August of 1954, NAA had extended the wingtips of the wing F-100C prototype by 12 inches, greatly improving the plane's roll characteristics.

As warning signs went unheeded, it was not a question if disaster would beset the flight test program, but rather a question of when. Disaster came beckoning on the morning of 12 October 1954, when George Welch was slated to demonstrate a maximum-G symmetrical pull-up at 23,700 feet during the fighter's highest possible Mach-number dive. This was the ultimate test for the Hun, stressing the airframe to its maximum capacity. If the F-100 survived and handled the severe flight loading reasonably well, there would be no more room for doubting the fighter's prowess.

Welch fired up the Hun, taxied out, called for clearance, and was airborne at 1046 hours. At precisely 1100, Welch was 45,000 feet above the Mojave Desert preparing for the test. As an audience was assembling below for the spectacle, a low-flying Boeing B-47 Stratojet crew also spotted the Hun as they were passing through 25,000 feet. Welch then began his dive, quickly gaining speed and momentum. A few seconds later, the glistening lines of the accelerating aircraft exploded into a bright orange and black plume. The B-47 crew immediately reported the incident and tried to ascertain if there was a survivor.

One good parachute was reported. Then a second parachute was reported. The aircraft's drogue chute had deployed during the catastrophic accident. Two other NAA test pilots, Bob Baker and Bud Pogue, rushed to

Welch's aid as he descended. Welch hit the ground—he was still alive. However, Welch had been mortally wounded—suffering tremendous gashes from chunks of metal striking his body when the cockpit of the plummeting fighter disintegrated around him. The beautiful silver F-100A was now only wreckage consisting mainly of tiny pieces. Adding insult to injury, these finite pieces of Super Sabre were strewn over acres of high desert.

AFTERMATH

NAA engineers soon began picking up the pieces of the catastrophe. As with all NAA test aircraft, this one was also heavily laden with test flight instruments. A camera that was placed facing the tail section of the aircraft during the fight was recovered in reasonably good condition. The film was promptly developed, revealing some startling insight to the accident. The shadow of the vertical stabilizer was shown racing horizontally, indicating a violent yaw took place induced by tail flutter. More film showed an oscillograph recording the motion of the entire aircraft during the yawing incident.

After diligent review, it was determined that Welch's F-100A had encountered the then-new phenomenon known as inertia roll coupling.

INERTIA ROLL COUPLING

Inertia roll coupling is the most complex of coupling instabilities, and is caused by a heavy but highly maneuverable aircraft's angle of attack and distribution of mass as it rolls through several revolutions. This phenomenon was first experienced with devastating results during air force pilot Mel Apt's test flight of the Bell X-2. This ill-fated encounter led to the complete destruction of the test aircraft along with the loss of Mel Apt's life. Little was known then about the destructive nature of the phenomenon. At that time, aeronautical technology was achieving quantum leaps every few months, and the flight envelope was continuously being pushed farther forward as each new aeronautical wonder took center stage.

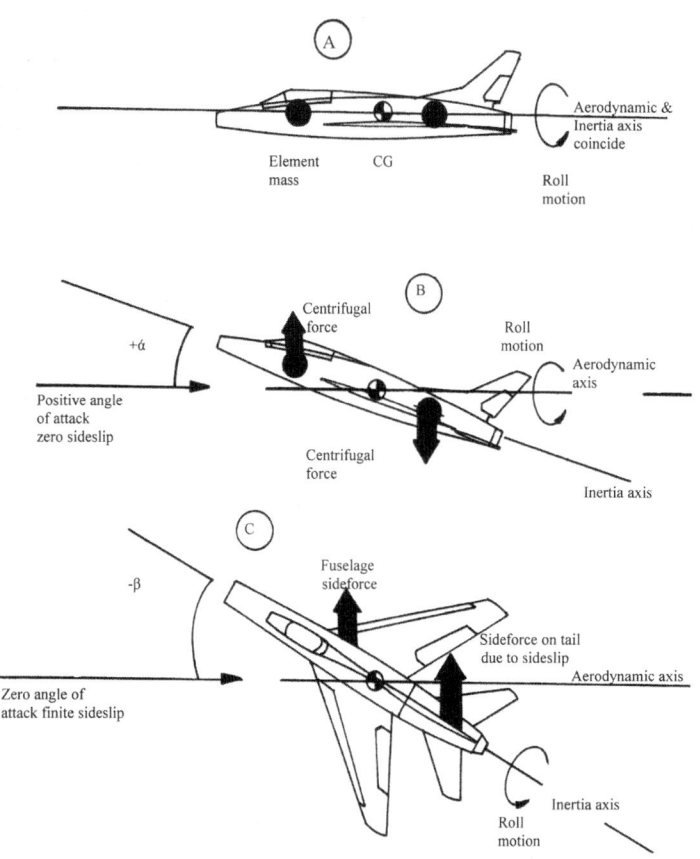

This diagram notes how inertia coupling for the F-100A manifested itself by inadequacies inherent in its overall design, especially in its vertical stabilizer. Condition A represents the F-100 in a relatively stable flight condition. The inertia axis and the aerodynamic axis are aligned; therefore, no subsequent inertia coupling would result from an instantaneous rolling motion. When the inertia axis becomes included in the aerodynamic axis, rotation about the aerodynamic axis would create centrifugal forces and cause a pitching moment. When this transpires, a rolling motion induces a pitching moment, whose delineation is accomplished through the action of proper aerodynamic moments. This, in fact, is inertia coupling and is illustrated in Figure B. Conversely, when the aircraft is rotated about the inertia axis, no inertia coupling presides, but the presence of aerodynamic coupling is prevalent. This is illustrated in Figure C, denoting an F-100 after rolling 90 degrees about the inertia axis. What was once the angle of attack is now the angle of sideslip. Of particular note, the original zero sideslip has now become zero angle of attack.

Because of modern aircraft design evolution, it was only a question of when inertia roll coupling would rear its ugly head. This was due in part to the continuous and ongoing aerodynamic refinements as well as a change in aircraft inertia requirements achieved to maintain high-speed flight characteristics.

The term coupling refers to some disturbance about one aircraft axis, which in turn, effects or disrupts the stability of the aircraft through another axis. An example of an uncoupled event occurring on an aircraft is when the elevator is displaced in the up or down position, thus affecting the aircraft pitch but not affecting it in yaw or roll altitude.

An example of a coupled motion could stem from a rudder displacement right or left. The ensuing motion could embrace some combination of yawing and a rolling motion. Therefore, the respective yawing and rolling motions combined define the resulting motion. This motion is relative to the aerodynamic forces interacting on the control surfaces and characterizes the term "aerodynamic coupling."

The inertia characteristics of the entire aircraft can be separated into the pitch, yaw, and roll inertia, which, in essence, is a direct measure of the resistance to the rolling, pitching, or yawing acceleration of the aircraft. Inertia coupling can be visualized by placing the entire mass of the aircraft in two strategic places, one representing the mass ahead of the aircraft's center of gravity (CG) and one behind it. There are two principal axis systems in play: (1) the aerodynamic or wind axis transmitting through the aircraft's CG in the direction of the relative airflow; and (2) the inertia axis also passing through the CG, in the direction of the two masses. Refer to the illustration for further understanding.

It is important to note that the initial inclination of the inertia axis above the aerodynamic axis will cause the inertia couple to initiate adverse yaw accompanied by a rolling motion. For instance, if the inertia axis were locally inclined below the aerodynamic axis, then the roll-induced couple would promote perverse yaw. Therefore, roll coupling often presents a problem at both positive and negative inertia axis inclinations. This greatly depends on the exact aerodynamic and inertia characteristic of the aircraft's configuration.

As a result of the rolling motion initiated by the aerodynamic and inertia coupling effect, a great variety of longitudinal, directional, and lateral forces accompanied by moments are, in fact, induced. The resultant aircraft motion is determined by a dominant and complex combination of aerodynamic forces augmented by inertia coupling. All aircraft, no matter what flight speed, exhibit some form of aerodynamic and inertia coupling, but at varying degrees. Roll coupling poses no problem as long as the moments produced by inertia coupling are counterbalanced by aerodynamic moments. A high-speed aircraft with a short wingspan and aspect ratio, accompanied with high roll ratio (F-100 roll rate was 200 degrees per second) is a breeding ground for the ill effects of inertia coupling. This is further supplemented by the increasing Mach numbers in aircraft, which allow for larger inclinations of the inertia axis with respect to the aerodynamic axis. This phenomenon allows for the further proportion of the inertial couple. Also of particular concern are the restoring aerodynamic moments, which deteriorate because of increasing Mach number and angle of attack. This adds greatly to the roll coupling tendency.

Because roll coupling intersects pitching and yawing motion, the longitudinal and directional stability of the aircraft is of paramount importance. These inherent characteristics are important in also determining the overall characteristics of the coupled motion. In accordance to the laws of aerodynamics, a stable aircraft, when disrupted in flight, especially in the pitch and yaw axis, will return to its state of equilibrium after a few oscillations. In each flight mode, the aircraft will display a coupled pitch-yaw frequency between the uncoupled and separate yaw and pitch frequencies. It has been found that the greater the static longitudinal and directional stability of the aircraft, the higher the coupled pitch-yaw frequency. For example, when an aircraft is subjected to a rolling motion, the acting inertia couple disrupts the aircraft in pitch and yaw, and with each roll revolution it also distributes a disrupting force function. Depending on the aerodynamic and physical characteristics of the aircraft—and, if they are just right—the aircraft could roll at a rate equal to the coupled pitch-yaw frequency present and the produced oscillatory motion would, in fact, diverge to some maximum amplitude to stabilize the aircraft.

The longitudinal stability of a typical high-speed military aircraft is far more important than the direction stability, which often results in a pitch frequency greater than the yaw frequency. The solution lies in the increase in direction stability by increasing the vertical stabilizer area, as was in the case of the F-100. After the

A view of the difference between the short-tail and tail-finned F-100As. *USAF via David W. Menard*

accident, the fighter's total vertical fin area was increased by 27 percent and its wingspan to 38.78 feet, thus restoring its direction and longitudinal stability overcoming its tendency for inertia roll coupling.

Uncoupled yawing frequency is lower than the pitch frequency, which translates, in a divergent condition attaining critical proportions first in yaw ushered in behind it by the pitch. It is a matter of conjecture whether the aircraft's motion approaches divergence directionally or longitudinally, and is best left for the theoreticians to determine.

Another type of roll coupling is referred to as autorotive rolling. This condition exists when a rolling aircraft encounters a large, perverse sideslip, due to the inertia couple and the rolling moment encumbered by the sideslip, and may exceed the bonds of lateral control. In order to offset this condition, the wing would be located high on the fuselage with a high sweepback position, or there would be a very large vertical stabilizer.

Depending on what type of flight condition is prevalent, there are four basic types of aircraft behavior that could exist under the influence of inertia roll coupling. They are:

1. Coupled motion—stable, but unstable. The flight motion is stable, but could result in aircraft-control loss or structural failure due to the inadequate damping of the motion.

2. Coupled motion—stable and acceptable. This condition results in a stable flight condition where the oscillation poses no threat to the control or structural integrity of the aircraft.

3. Coupled motion—divergent and unacceptable. This situation exists when the rate of divergence is too high and the pilot cannot respond to it in time to prevent a catastrophe.

4. Coupled motion—divergent, but acceptable. In this particular condition, the rate of divergence is slow enough so that the pilot can react to it in time to initiate corrective action.

There are several strategies to deal with inertia roll coupling. The following items are viable solutions:

Increase directional stability.

Reduce the dihedral effect of the wing.

Minimize the flight inclination of the inertia axis during normal flight modes.

Reduce any undesirable aerodynamic coupling.

Eliminate the roll rate, roll duration, and angle of attack or the aircraft load factor in anticipation of roll maneuvers.

Items (a) through (d) are primarily influenced during the design phase of the aircraft. Item (e) is effected by imposing limitation on roll maneuvers. These restrictions should be noted in the flight manual of the aircraft.

Because of this deadly encounter with inertia-roll coupling, major design changes for the F-100A ensued. North American started by increasing the vertical tail area by 27 percent, delaying the onset of instability above Mach 1.4. The aspect ratio of the F-100's wings was also increased. Thirdly, the wingtips were extended to increase the overall wingspan and area in accordance with the modified aspect ratio. This was also initiated to move the wing center of pressure aft to compensate

This is the third production F-100A undergoing maintenance. Notice the FW 757 in the background sporting a taller vertical stabilizer. *Courtesy San Diego Aerospace Museum*

for a change in center of gravity. This change was due, in part, to the change in the engine's CG. These inherent and much-needed changes increased the wingspan from 36.78 feet to 38.78 feet, and increased the wing area from 376 square feet to 385.21 square feet. As a result, all existing F-100A models built, and being built, underwent these changes.

The first three F-100As modified were extensively tested by USAF, NAA, and NACA personnel. As a direct result of North American's efforts, vast amounts of data on supersonic flight stability and control were compiled, placing North American at an advantage over other defense contractors and aircraft companies in the United States. At the behest of Raymond H. Rice, vice president of engineering at North American, special documents on this topic were prepared and distributed to all active aircraft companies in the United States.

PERFORMANCE

What follows are notes on flight characteristics of the different models of the F-100. These comments reflect data that was collected from the flight testing of the F-100.

FLIGHT CHARACTERISTICS FOR F-100A AND C: Both the A and C models handled satisfactorily throughout their flight and speed envelopes. When operated at normal speeds, the aircraft provided a stable platform for gunning and ordnance. However, adverse yaw was encountered at high angles of attack.

An early F-100A initiates a loop, or the beginnings of one, for the onlooking photographer. *Courtesy Jay Miller Aviation History Collection*

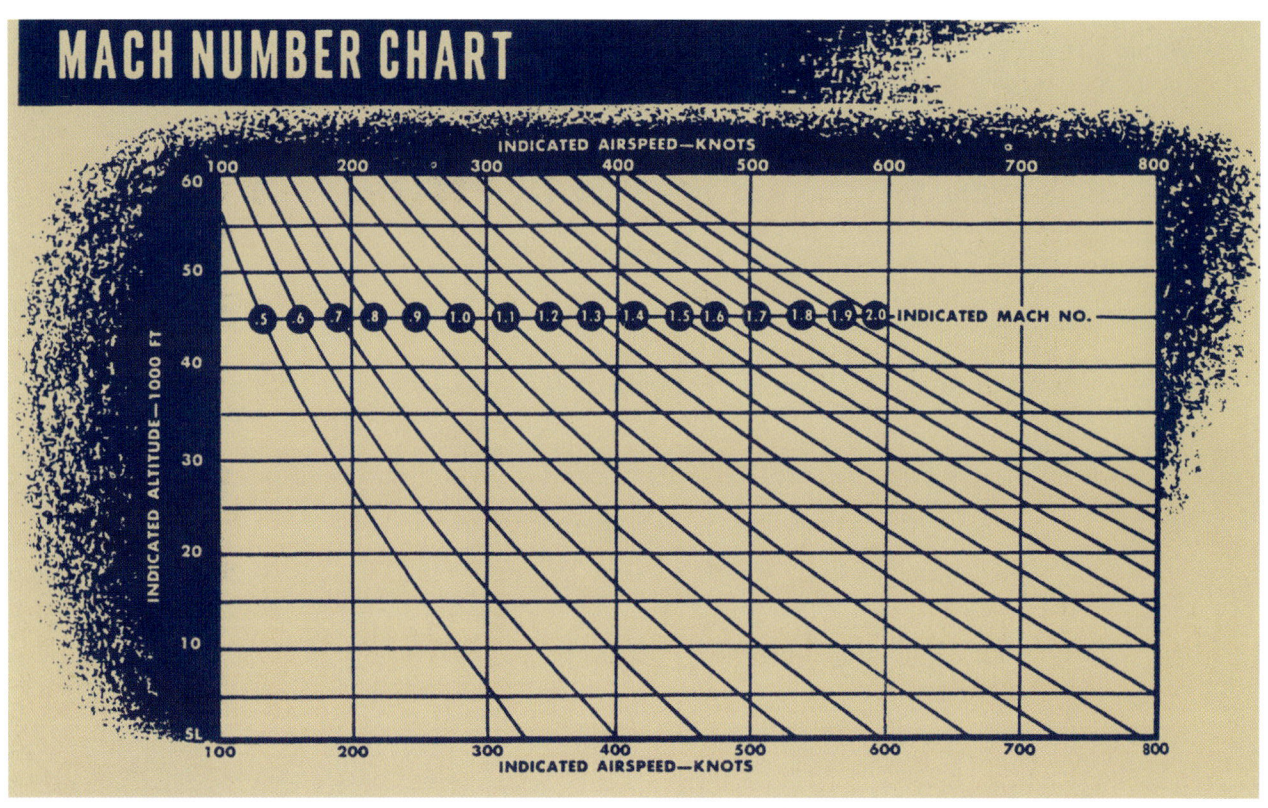

Above: This is a Mach number chart, and it was used quite frequently among F-100 pilots. It is governed by altitude versus indicated air speed.

Below: This photograph clearly depicts four F-100As of the 479th FDW flying loose formation. *Courtesy Jay Miller Aviation History Collection*

MACH NUMBER: Mach number provided a convenient speed index for flight characteristics possessed by the Hun. The Mach number index eliminated the need of remembering a long list of indicated air speeds for various altitudes. A certain flight characteristic appeared at the same Mach number at any altitude and varied only by intensity. For example, the lower the altitude, the higher the indicated airspeed for a given Mach number. This meant greater air pressure was exerted at lower altitudes.

STALLING AND MINIMUM CONTROL SPEEDS: Because the F-100 Super Sabre embodied a highly sweptback wing, it did not possess a clearly defined stall. Instead, when a particularly low air speed was reached, in general the pilot felt mild stick forces accompanied by a mild buffeting. When these events occurred, they were usually accompanied by an increase in descent rate and an extra control effort demonstrated by the pilot. This was attributed to the left wingtip stalling out, resulting in a forward movement in the center of pressure.

The speed at which control efforts became excessive was deemed the minimum control speed. For an F-100 topping out at 25,000 pounds gross weight with power

A 118th TFS F-100A cruises over its home state of Connecticut. *Courtesy Jay Miller Aviation History Collection*

F-100C s/n 54-2099 has her slats clearly extended for this stunning camera shot. *Courtesy Jay Miller Aviation History Collection*

AIRSPEED LIMITATIONS

700 KNOTS IAS WHEN CARRYING:
  a. NO EXTERNAL LOAD.

670 KNOTS IAS WHEN CARRYING:
  a. PYLON ADAPTER OR LAUNCHER ADAPTER AT ONE OR BOTH ORDNANCE STATIONS.

600 KNOTS IAS WHEN CARRYING:
  a. TYPE II OR NAA TYPE III DROP TANKS EMPTY.
  b. PYLON OR PYLON-AIM-9B MISSILE * COMBINATION INSTALLED AT ONE ORDNANCE STATION. (Do not exceed Mach 1.2.)
  c. PYLON OR PYLON-AIM-9B MISSILE * COMBINATION INSTALLED AT TWO ORDNANCE STATIONS. (Do not exceed Mach 1.4.)
  d. 750 LB BOMBS (Do not exceed Mach .90 below 10,000 feet, Mach .95 between 10,000 and 25,000 feet, and Mach 1.0 above 25,000 feet.)
  e. TYPE XA LAUNCHER AT EACH INBOARD STATION (with or without AGM-12B missile on either or both launchers.) Do not exceed Mach 1.4.

NOTE
With only one Type XA launcher installed (with or without an AGM-12B missile on the launcher), do not exceed Mach .90.

550 KNOTS WHEN CARRYING:
  a. M65A1 OR M64A1 BOMBS. (Do not exceed Mach .90 below 10,000 feet, Mach .95 between 10,000 feet and 25,000 feet, or Mach 1.0 above 25,000 feet.)

500 KNOTS IAS WHEN CARRYING:
  a. NAA TYPE III DROP TANKS WITH FUEL.
  b. FIRE BOMBS. (Do not exceed Mach .95 below 25,000 feet or Mach 1.0 above 25,000 feet.)

450 KNOTS IAS WHEN CARRYING:
  a. TYPE II DROP TANKS WITH FUEL.

NOTE
Do not exceed Mach .95 with Type II drop tanks.

*Limits also apply if TDU-11/B target rocket is substituted for a missile on one or both pylons.

This is a list of limiting conditions responsible for variations in the F-100A and C air speed.

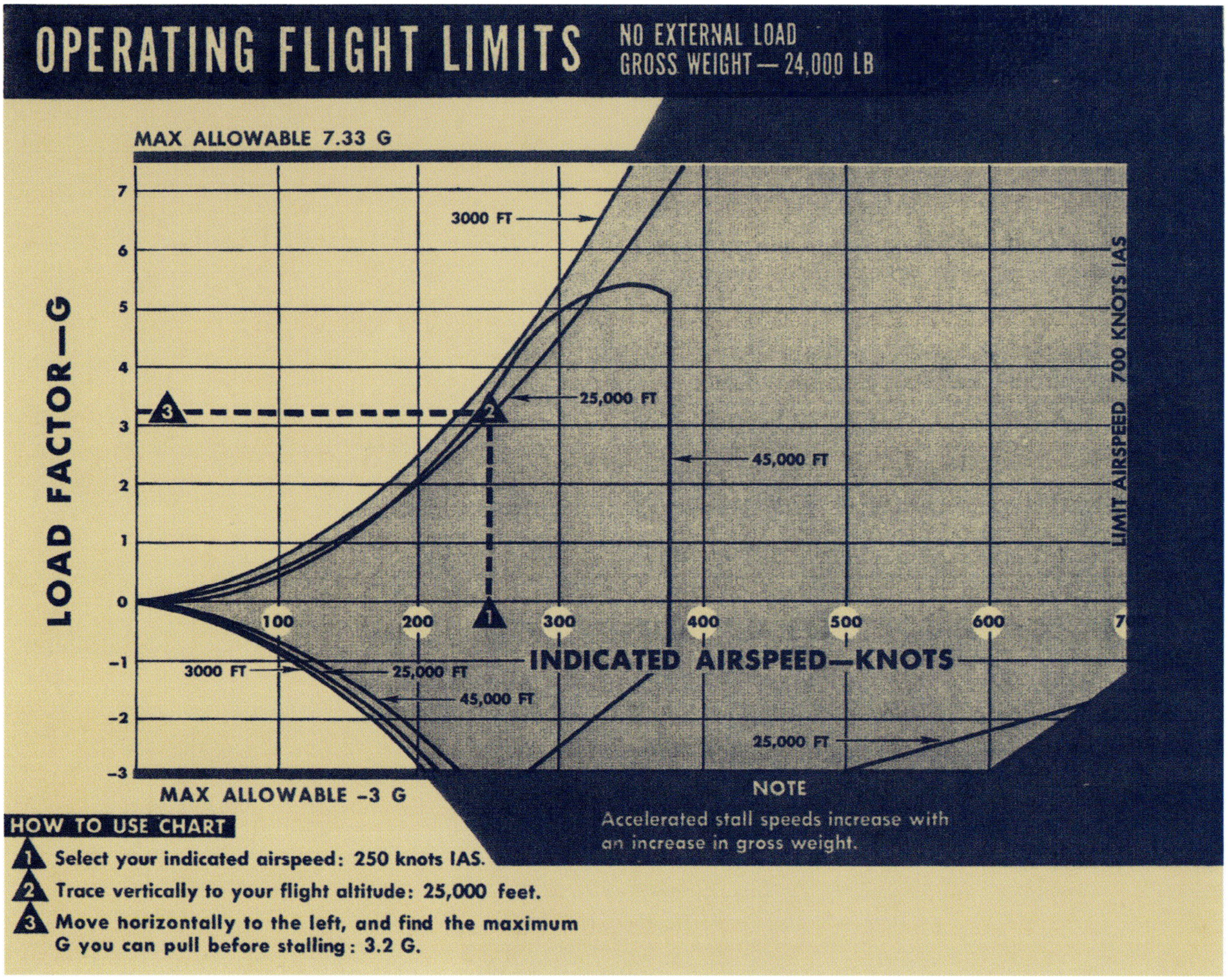

OPERATING FLIGHT LIMITS — NO EXTERNAL LOAD / GROSS WEIGHT — 24,000 LB

MAX ALLOWABLE 7.33 G

[Chart: Load Factor—G (vertical axis, −3 to 7) vs. Indicated Airspeed—Knots (horizontal axis, 100 to 700). Curves shown for 3000 FT, 25,000 FT, and 45,000 FT. Right side: LIMIT AIRSPEED 700 KNOTS IAS. Bottom: MAX ALLOWABLE −3 G.]

NOTE: Accelerated stall speeds increase with an increase in gross weight.

HOW TO USE CHART
1. Select your indicated airspeed: 250 knots IAS.
2. Trace vertically to your flight altitude: 25,000 feet.
3. Move horizontally to the left, and find the maximum G you can pull before stalling: 3.2 G.

Above: The air-speed limits for the Hun with no external load and in all approved external loading conditions are given in this table. This is an operating flight limits chart, which lists parameters dictated by the load factor rated in Gs, altitude, and indicated air speed.

Right: The tight formation flying of this four-ship flight of F-100Cs of the 479th FDW demonstrates how well the pilots were trained. *Courtesy Jay Miller Aviation History Collection*

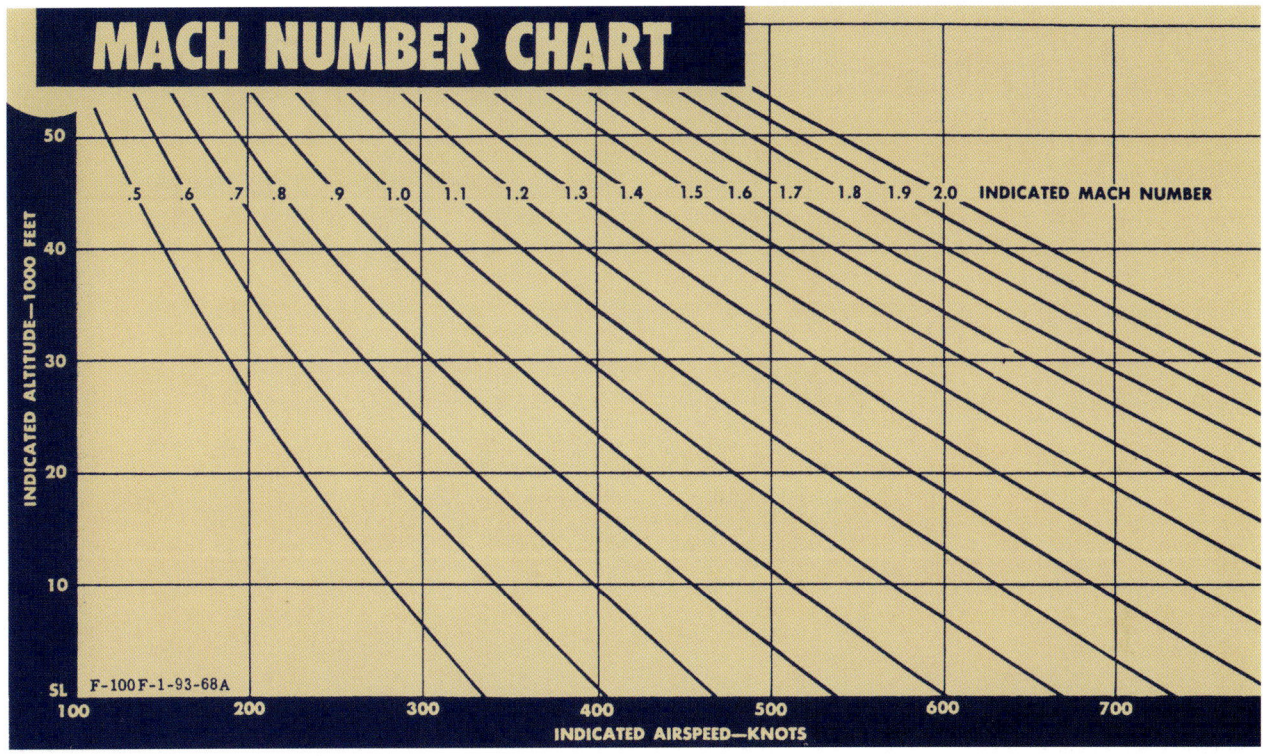

The Mach number chart exclusively used in the operation of the F-100D is very similar to the charts used for the F-100A and C.

off and landing gear fully extended, minimum control speed was determined to be 137 knots indicated air speed (IAS). If the speed was further reduced, the rate of descent increased, followed by a yawing and rolling tendency. For all practical purposes, the stall speed in the previously mentioned configuration was determined to occur at 131 knots IAS.

MAXIMUM ALLOWABLE AIR SPEED: The airspeed limits for the Hun with no external load and in all approved external loading conditions were based on four major components:

Aerodynamic stability of the aircraft when carrying external ordnance.

The structural integrity of the individual ordnance carried.

The structural integrity of the mounting.

The flutter characteristics of the entire ordnance configuration.

Any one or all factors could combine to determine the maximum allowable air speed.

FLIGHT CHARACTERISTICS FOR F-100D AND F: The F-100D and F-100F variants exhibited for the most part similar flight characteristics, except in the case of the F-100F's elongated fuselage, which resulted in higher aerodynamic yawing moments while in the spin configuration. The spin qualities and recovery techniques demonstrated by the F-100D and the F-100F for the most part were virtually the same.

A 429th TFS F-100D strokes its afterburner and begins its takeoff roll. *Doug Henderson via Jay Miller Aviation History Collection*

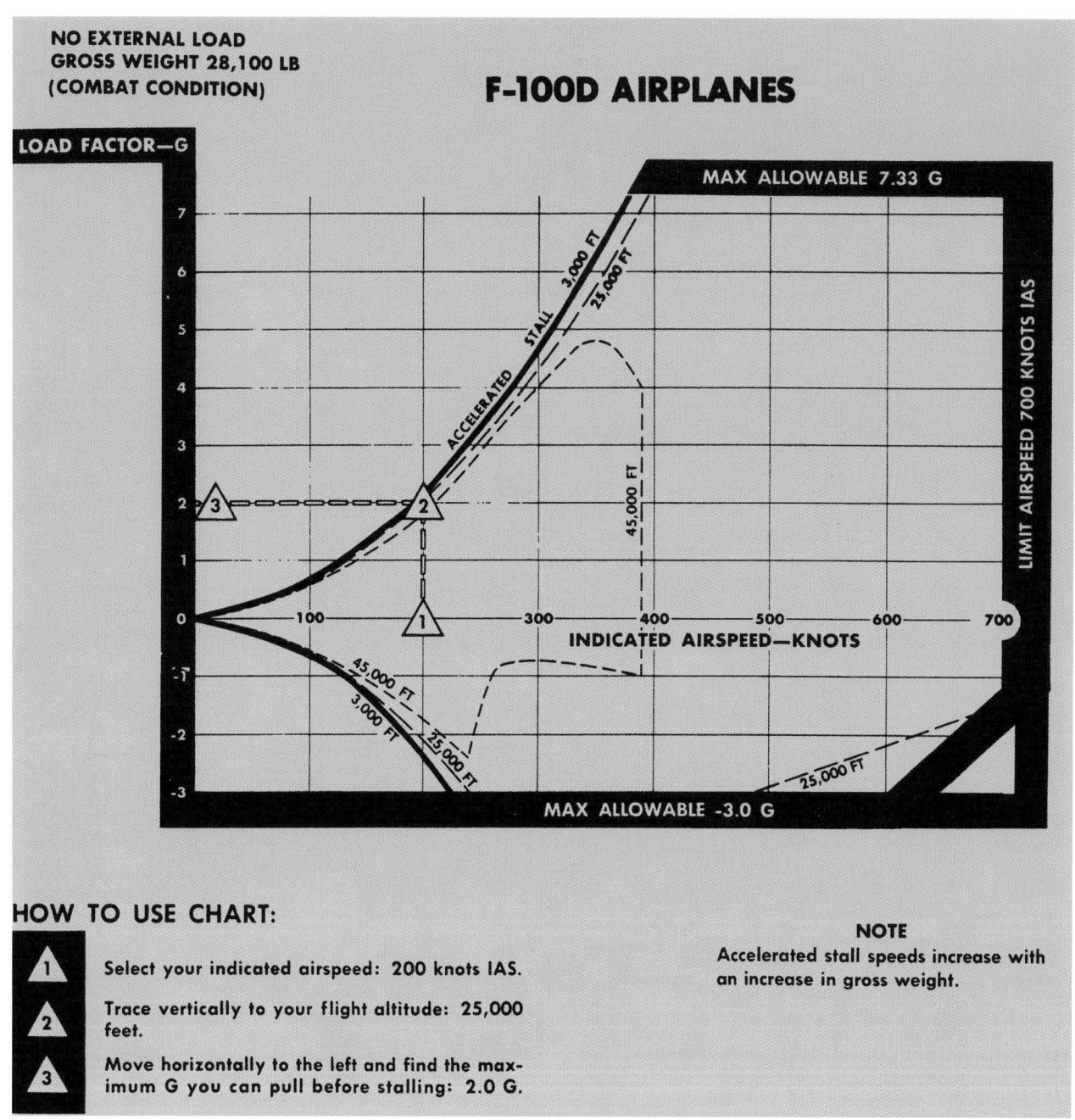

This chart outlines operational flight limitations for the F-100 Super Sabre. It is also governed by load factor in Gs, indicated air speed, and altitude.

FLIGHT CONTROL EFFECTIVENESS: The one-piece, all-moving horizontal stabilizer provided good overall maneuvering response throughout its subsonic to supersonic flight design. This was a new design concept that initiated good flight control in all flight conditions. Its response was phenomenal and far superior to conventional elevator stabilizer combinations embraced by the aeronautical community at that time. Its superior performance was particularly noticeable at low altitudes and at high speeds. The dynamic stabilizer was a primary reason why the artificial feel was designed into the F-100 control system so the pilot would avoid over-

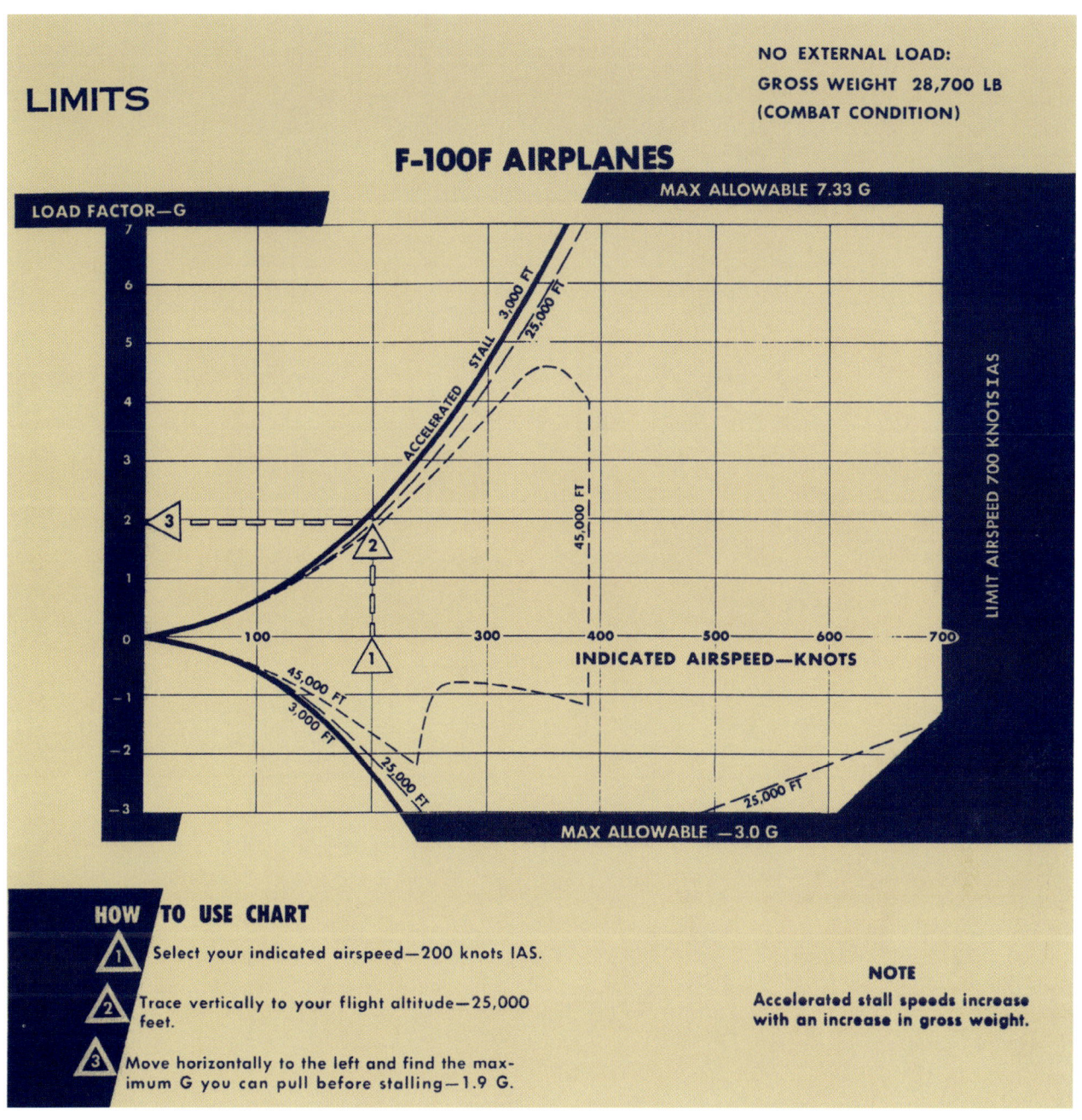

The flight limitation chart used exclusively for the F-100F Super Sabre was very similar to the charts used for the F-100A, C, and D.

controlling the fighter, thus dangerously overstressing the airframe.

Aircraft response was sluggish during low-speed flight and during landing, thus requiring more input to the control yoke, increasing stabilizer deflection. It was possible during these conditions to over-control the Hun, resulting in the control yoke stiffening up momentarily due to maximum demands made on the stabilizer actuator.

AILERON CONTROL: The inherent position of the ailerons situated farther inboard than conventional aileron installations minimized the inordinate wing twisting that resulted in lower roll rates. Because of this

Four F-100Ds en route to sea duty with a KC-135A mother ship. *Lt. Col. T. Barnes via David W. Menard*

fact, very high roll rates of 200 degrees per second could be obtained, and extreme caution was emphasized to the inexperienced pilot until thoroughly familiarized with the ailerons' effectiveness. Because of the Hun's tendency to yaw at low to mild transonic speeds, when coordinated turns were made at subsonic, transonic, and supersonic speeds, it was necessary to hold a slight opposite rudder in the turn. It was also possible to produce large adverse yaw angles, which developed at low to medium air speeds. If the ailerons were reversed too quickly following high-rate aileron rolls, the phenomenon would occur. When control inputs were applied correctly, this condition did not develop.

RUDDER CONTROL: The rudder gave relative and effective directional control at all normal flight speeds. The rudder's usefulness transcended the inherent instability that occurred at low air speeds with aircraft utilizing sweptback wings. The F-100's rudder provided sufficient control throughout the flight envelope under normal conditions.

FLAPS: The F-100D and F-100F were the only variants to incorporate a redesigned wing utilizing flaps. The wing flaps were quite effective in aiding control during low-speed flight. Not only were they her-

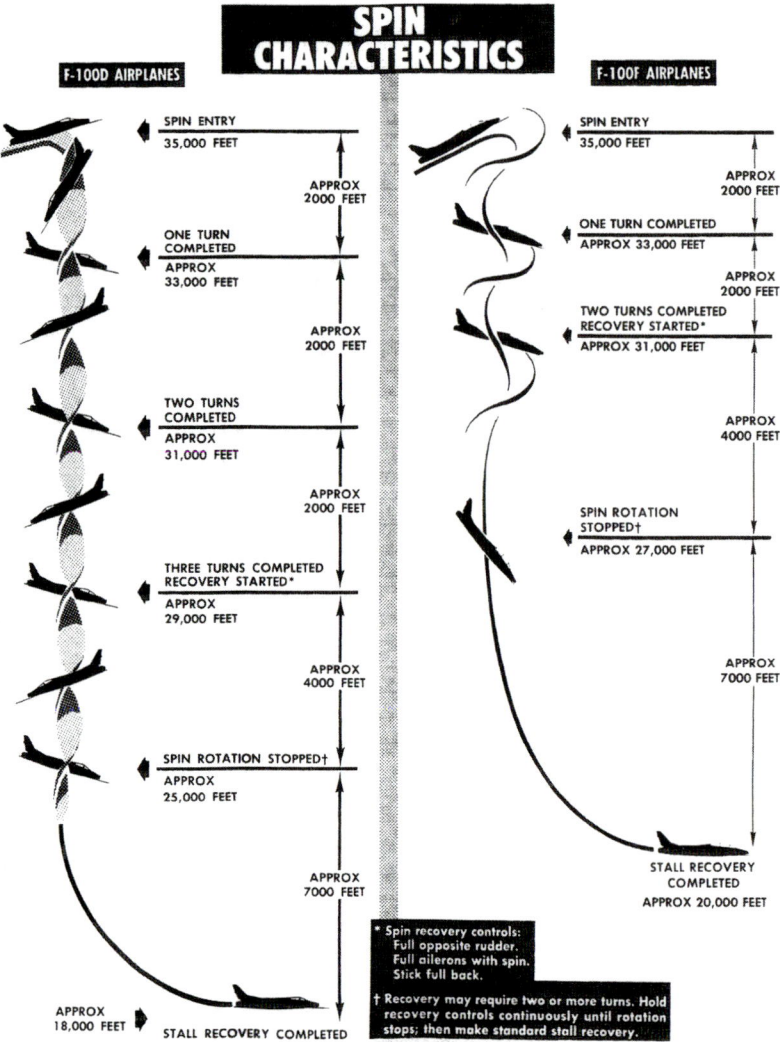

The spin characteristics for the F-100D and F consisted of several events, all encompassing several thousand feet for necessary recovery to occur.

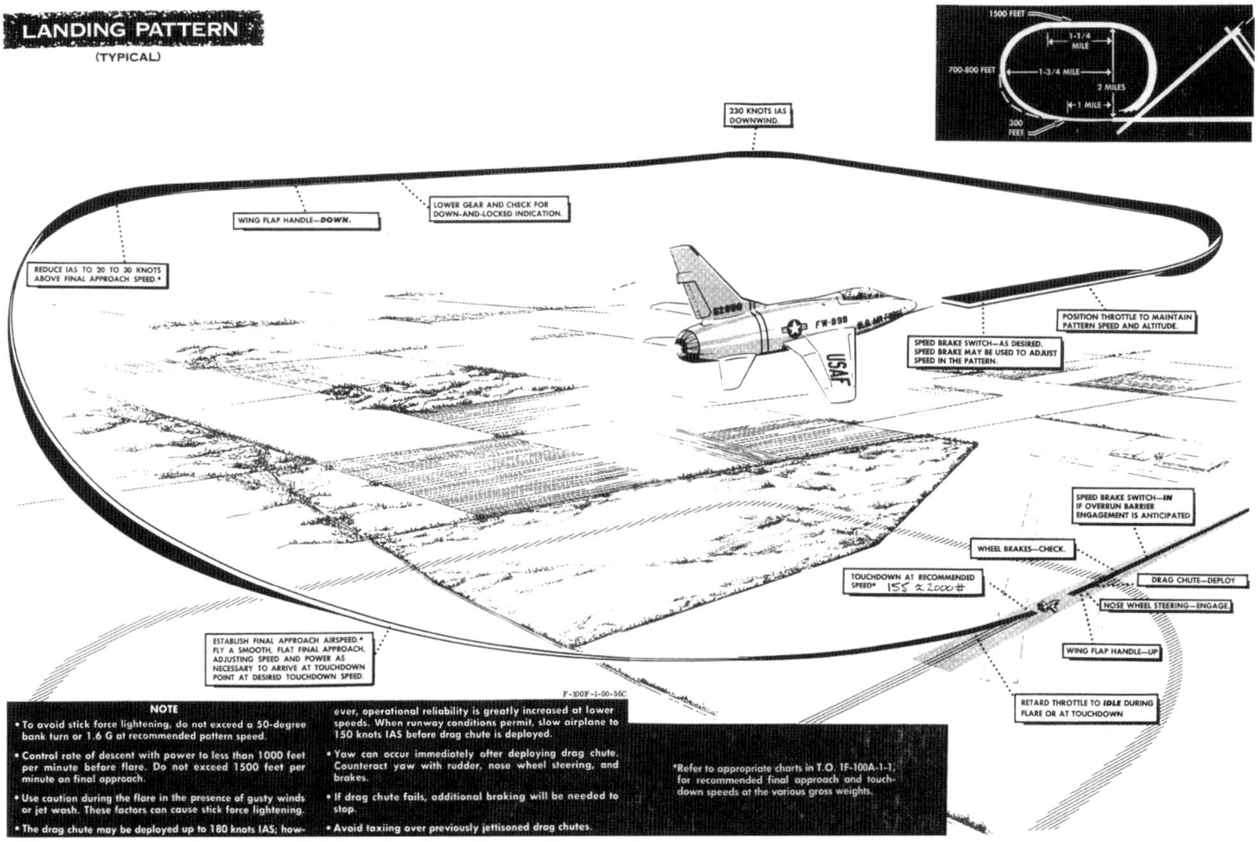

Understanding of landing procedures in the Hun was paramount, especially during flameouts or any sudden loss of power.

alded for their added low-speed control, the pilot enjoyed better visibility on landing approaches because lower nose-up altitudes were required. Some aerodynamic buffet was encountered, and during landing it was quickly rectified by automatic pitch correction. The automatic pitch, though, was not available when the flaps were lowered to the intermediate position.

SPEED BRAKE: The speed brake was very effective in creating a considerable amount of drag at all flight speeds without generating an inordinate amount of buffeting. Because of its well-thought-out design, only small trim changes were required during its use. It was noted that when the speed brake was employed at supersonic speeds, sight yawing of the fighter occurred. Mild buffeting was experienced when the speed brake and flaps were fully extended at the same time.

SLAT OPERATION: Wing leading slats were installed to improve flight performance at low, as well as high,

A 4758th Defense Systems Evaluation Squadron F-100C displays her Day-Glo orange external fuel tank high over the desert Southwest. *Courtesy Jay Miller Aviation History Collection*

Mach numbers. They also provided a decreased drag, aided maneuverability at high angles of attack, and delayed the onset of buffeting.

F-100F s/n 56-3733 in flight in its polished bare-metal finish. *USAF via David W. Menard*

The performance characteristics of all F-100 variants were quite good, and those who flew it found it to be exciting, exhilarating, and challenging, but nevertheless fast and fun to fly.

F-100 AND SKYRAY RECORD FLIGHTS

Douglas Aircraft Company in 1953, steadfast in its resolve for the flight testing of the Skyray, had found itself temporarily diverted from this task to focus its attention on achieving new speed records with the fledgling Skyray. In order to accomplish this task, Westinghouse made available its XJ40-WE-8 afterburning turbojet for immediate installation in Skyray prototype example 587.

After a series of minor setbacks, on 3 October 1953, Lt. Comdr. James Verdin set a new world absolute speed record of 753.4 mph in XF4D-1 587. This event transpired over Southern California's Salton Sea. Two weeks later, a different pilot, Robert Rahn, flew XF4D-1, example 587, to a new 100-kilometer closed course record of 728.1 miles per hour at Edwards Air Force Base. Special prepping performed on example 587 culminated in the extensive lightening of the aircraft and the total removal of its tail wheel bumper. This was necessary in order to attain the coveted speed records that they desired.

Soon, "Pete" Everest eclipsed this record in the YF-100 Super Sabre. On 29 October 1953 at Edwards Air Force Base he flew the first prototype YF-100A to a world speed record of 755.149 miles per hour. It was the last such record established at low altitude.

As a result of these speed records attained in part by the Skyray and the Super Sabre, special honors and the prestigious Collier trophy were bestowed on Douglas Chief Engineer Ed Heinemann for his involvement in the design of the Skyray and North American's James H. Kindelberger for his role in the Super Sabre's inception. This award is presented each year and represents for its recipients the greatest achievement in aviation to date. These two men graciously accepted the trophy on behalf of their efforts for developing the first supersonic aircraft to enter military service: the U.S. Air Force's F-100 Super Sabre and the U.S. Navy's F4D-1 Skyray.

F-100 VERSUS MIG-19

There is an argument that exists to this present day regarding which of the two aircraft, the F-100 or the MiG-19, was the superior. The only known confrontation between a Super Sabre and another aircraft was reported over the skies of South Vietnam regarding a MiG-17, with the Super Sabre emerging the victor. To date, no known confrontation ever existed between the F-100 and a MiG-19. Thus, the issue of which aircraft was superior is subject to speculation and conjecture. However, it is possible to draw some comparisons from each aircraft's strengths and weaknesses.

Both aircraft were designed as day fighters, exceeding Mach 1 in level flight. The MiG-19, although manufactured in greater numbers than the Hun, nevertheless achieved an abbreviated service life with the Soviet Union. It is thought to still be employed in North

CONDITIONS		*F-100A J57-P-7	*F-100C J57-P-39		*F-100C J57-P-21		**F-100D J57-P-21		**F-100F J57-P-21	
		Air Superiority Mission	Air Superiority Mission	Fighter-Bomber Mission	Air Superiority Mission	Fighter-Bomber Mission	Air Superiority Mission	Fighter-Bomber Mission	Air Superiority Mission	Fighter-Bomber Mission
TAKE-OFF WEIGHT	(lb)	28,971	32,536	34,828	32,615	34,907	33,691	36,003	34,235	36,547
Fuel at 6.5 lb/gal (grade JP-4)	(lb)	8483	11,050	11,050	11,050	11,050	11,297	11,297	11,297	11,297
Payload (ammunition)	(lb)	770	560	560	560	560	560	560	245	245
Payload (bombs)	(lb)	—	—	2000	—	2000	—	2000	—	2000
Wing Loading	(lb/sq ft)	75.2	84.5	90.5	84.8	90.8	84.2	90.0	85.4	91.3
Stall speed (power off)	(kn)	138	146	150	147	151	146	151	147	152
Take-off ground run at SL ①	(ft)	2970	3750	4300	3200	3850	3350	3900	3480	4010
Take-off to clear 50 ft ①	(ft)	4670	5800	6650	4590	5200	4970	5620	5130	5770
Rate of climb at SL ②	(fpm)	5000	4200	3800	4600	3700	4300	3650	4230	3600
Time: SL to 20,000 ft ②	(min)	4.5	5.4	7.0	5.1	5.9	5.5	6.3	5.4	6.4
Time: SL to 30,000 ft ②	(min)	7.3	8.5	12.9	8.9	11.7	9.9	12.7	9.4	13.3
Service ceiling (100 fpm) ②	(ft)	41,100	38,800	35,800	38,700	34,200	38,000	34,300	37,600	33,300
COMBAT RADIUS	(n mi)	402	541	514	577	543	564	531	555	528
Average speed	(kn)	512	510	503	510	505	510	505	510	505
Initial cruising altitude	(ft)	37,700	35,600	28,900	35,600	32,400	35,000	31,400	34,600	30,900
Final cruising altitude	(ft)	44,000	42,800	41,500	43,800	42,400	43,000	41,600	42,600	41,200
Total mission time	(hr)	2.00	2.56	2.25	2.70	2.39	2.64	2.34	2.61	2.33
COMBAT WEIGHT	(lb)	24,716	27,237	27,062	27,161	27,036	28,177	27,781	28,746	28,307
Combat altitude	(ft)	35,000	35,000	SL	35,000	SL	35,000	SL	35,000	SL
Combat speed ①	(kn)	742	716	644	805	643	795	652	798	651
Combat climb ①	(fpm)	9500	8500	20,300	9500	21,200	8900	21,500	8800	21,000
Combat ceiling (500 fpm) ①	(ft)	51,200	49,300	49,000	49,500	49,200	48,900	49,100	48,400	48,700
Service ceiling (100 fpm) ②	(ft)	45,100	43,500	42,900	43,500	43,100	43,200	43,500	42,700	43,000
Max rate of climb at SL ①	(fpm)	24,000	21,800	20,300	20,800	21,200	21,100	21,500	20,700	21,000
Max speed at 35,000 ft ①	(kn)	742	716	620	805	724	795	797	798	800
Basic speed ①	(kn/ft)	—	—	644/SL	—	643/SL	—	652/SL	—	651/SL
LANDING WEIGHT	(lb)	20,936	22,171	22,916	22,250	22,957	23,124	23,572	23,668	24,133
Ground roll at SL	(ft)	3850	4020	4140	4030	4150	3530	3590	3600	3660
Ground roll (auxiliary brake)	(ft)	2320	2470	2550	2480	2550	2210	2270	2250	2310
Total from 50 ft	(ft)	5190	5440	5570	5450	5580	4840	4920	4920	5000
Total from 50 ft (auxiliary brake)	(ft)	3740	3870	4000	3900	4000	3530	3590	3600	3660

① MAXIMUM POWER
② MILITARY POWER
*BASED ON FLIGHT TEST DATA
**BASED ON F-100C FLIGHT TEST DATA

NORTH AMERICAN AVIATION, INC. INTERNATIONAL AIRPORT LOS ANGELES 45, CALIFORNIA

NA-57-1413 PAGE 43

A performance summary chart of all F-100 models.

Korea. The Super Sabre found prominence as a potent fighter-bomber and shouldered yeoman's duty admirably in Vietnam.

As to who would be the better dogfighter of the two would rest in the skill of the combating pilot. The MiG-19 had a better thrust-to-weight ratio (TWR) through the advent of its Klimov RD-9B turbojets and a significantly lighter air frame. Conversely, it is believed the F-100 could out-turn its MiG counterpart and possessed a better weapons array. The MiG-19 packed adequate firepower employing its 30mm cannon, but its AA-1 alkali beam-riding missiles were not as effective as the Hun's infrared-guided AIM-9 Sidewinders.

The speed of the MiG-19 and F-100 were roughly the same, but the combat TWR was different, .89 for the MiG-19 and .62 for the F-100D. As a result of their varied weight, their wing loading was vastly different. The MiG-19 employing its lighter airframe sported a wing loading of 59 lb/ft2 versus 72 lb/ft2 for the F-100. The MiG-19, because of its design, inherited short legs so to speak. It possessed short-range capabilities, and even augmented with wing tanks it still maintained poor endurance. The MiG-19's sole intent resided in that of an interceptor. On the other hand, the heavier Hun in the hands of a skilled pilot would probably emerge the victor, and was far more adaptable than the MiG-19.

A very gaudy "Pattern Ship" based at McClellan Air Force Base, California, in the mid-1960s. *Courtesy Jay Miller Aviation History Collection*

CHAPTER FOUR

F-100 MODELS

THE SUPER SABRE WAS OFFERED in four distinct and varying models. Apart from the YF-100A, the Hun evolved into the F-100A, F-100C, F-100D and, finally, the two-seat and trainer version F-100F. The F-100B later departed on its own developmental program, subsequently evolving into the North American F-107A interceptor. This variation's vast potential was never fully realized due to the U.S. Air Force's selection of the Republic F-105 Thunderchief.

F-100A

The F-100A was built as a single-place, supersonic air-superiority fighter powered by a Pratt & Whitney J57 axial-flow turbojet engine with an afterburner. This design sported a 45-degree sweptback wing including automatic leading-edge slats and two-section inboard-located ailerons. The horizontal stabilizer was a one-piece unit operated by the pilot through a hydraulically actuated, irreversible control system.

The design intent for the F-100A was to be geometrically identical to the sculpted dimensions of the YF-100A prototype. As fate had it, the F-100A was slightly altered due to the flawed discretion of a select group of NAA engineers. Despite significant design changes that developed, the F-100A never measured up to the air-superiority fighter that the air force wanted. It was ascertained in late 1955, through project Hot Rod initiated by the air force, that the F-100A demonstrated great performance but still possessed fundamental functional and operational deficiencies. Total phase-out of the F-100A from U.S. Air Force inventory began in late 1958.

The fourth production F-100A was used for ordnance testing, and carried two bombs painted for the same.
Courtesy Jay Miller Aviation History Collection

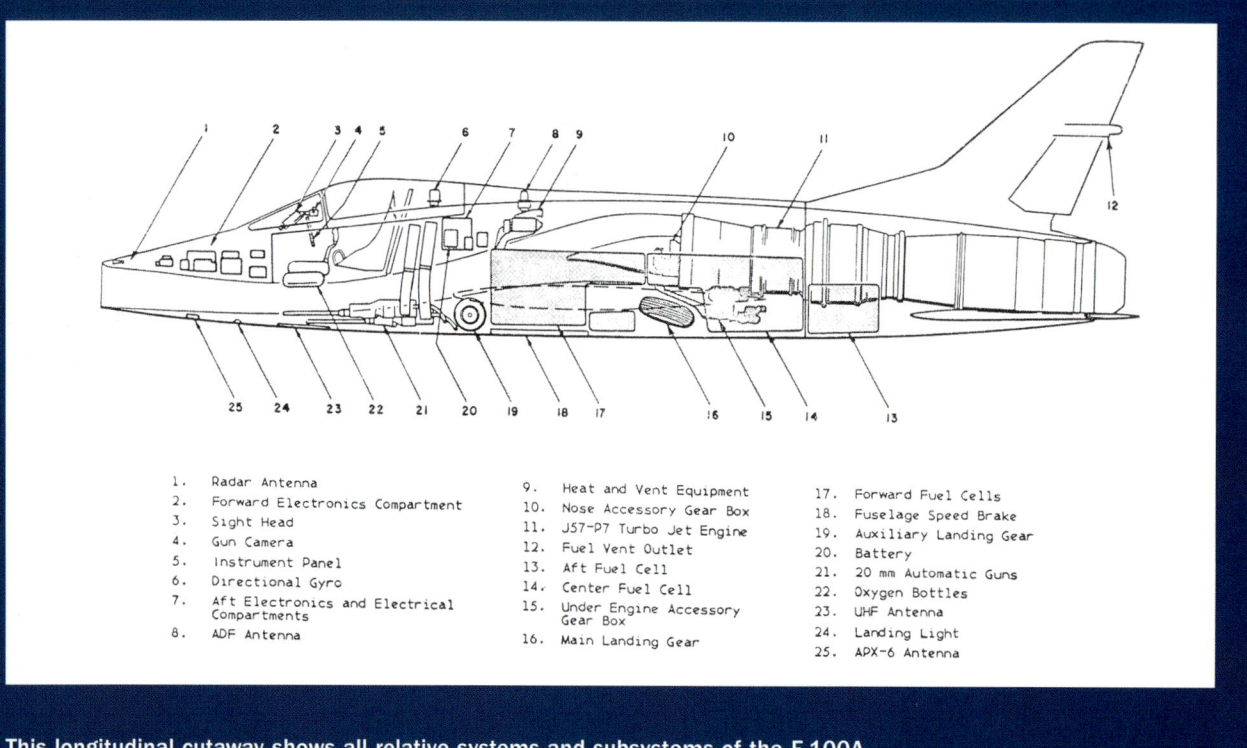

This longitudinal cutaway shows all relative systems and subsystems of the F-100A.

F-100C

The F-100C was identical in almost all respects to the A version except for redesigned wings. The F-100C incorporated a wet wing, meaning fuel cells were added inside the wing structure, eliminating the need for conventional fuel tanks and increasing fuel capacity. After the YF-100A's first flight, the air force asked NAA to study the possibility of increasing the Hun's fuel capacity with the wet-wing concept. From the onset of the initial F-100A design, the air force wanted it to hold more fuel, leading to the advent of the F-100C.

In addition to the fuel cells, the C-model's wing carried reinforcing for hard points to carry added munitions. Further strengthening of the wing to carry additional external ordnance reflected the air force's desire to transform the Hun to a fighter-bomber.

F-100C s/n 53-1712 in flight over a mountain range in Southern California. *Courtesy David W. Menard*

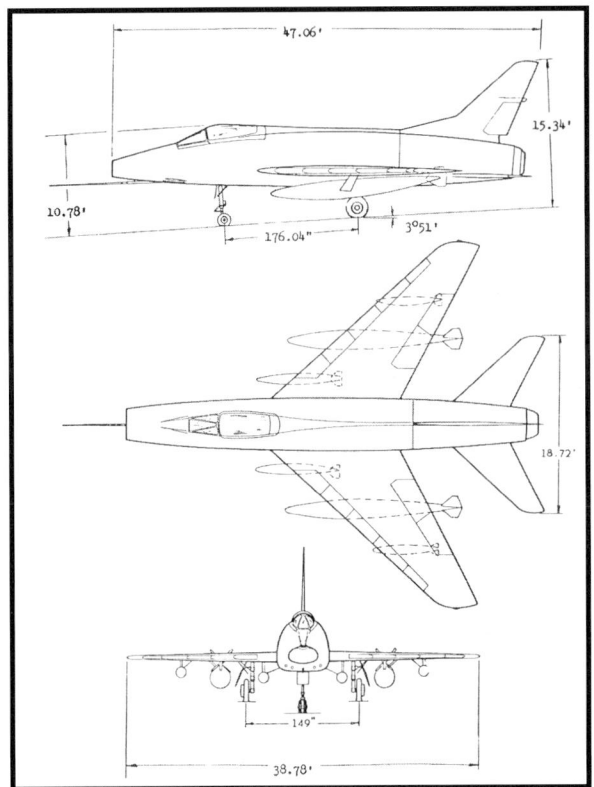

Above: This is how the F-100C cockpit tub and instrument panel appear to an entering pilot. Notice the rudder pedals and control yoke located in the bottom edge of the picture. *Courtesy Jay Miller Aviation History Collection*

Left: A three-view of the F-100C Super Sabre variant.

Provisions were also made to incorporate the use of in-flight refueling capabilities in the F-100C.

Because of this new wet-wing requirement, North American engineers redistributed the wing's integral systems to make room for the added fuel cells and devised a novel approach for the effective sealing of the tanks. All of the bolts that fastened the skin to the spars were sealed with the high-pressure insertion (at 7,000 psi) of a special material into a series of holes. The strategic location of these holes enabled the sealant to be channeled through a groove cut in the spar. This was necessary in order for the sealant to flow into any space created by the slight deflection of the wings under the added load of external stores and normal flight conditions. The new wing structure could hold, utilizing its six underwing stations, a variety of ordnance, some of

This F-100C on a landing roll has been fitted with an F-100D vertical tail. *Courtesy Jay Miller Aviation History Collection*

An engineless F-100D sits in limbo awaiting restoration somewhere in Texas. *Courtesy Jay Miller Aviation History Collection*

An F-100D s/n 55-2780 awaits further flights. *Courtesy David W. Menard Collection*

which included external tanks carrying up to 2,000 pounds in fuel, a dozen 5-inch high-velocity aircraft rockets (HVARs), and provisions for nuclear munitions.

In light of these modifications, the F-100C encountered slight longitudinal instability caused by the additional pair of 200-gallon fuel tanks used to supplement the 275-gallon pair already in use. This problem was later solved by switching to a pair of 335-gallon tanks. The F-100C could carry two 450-gallon wing tanks as well. To round off the design changes, Pratt & Whitney had upgraded and improved its J57-P-7 with their newest J57-P-21 axial-flow turbojet, increasing the Hun's overall speed by 35 knots.

TAC F-100D s/n 55-3712 with 450-gallon external fuel tanks and 1960-vintage IFR boom fitted. *Lt. Col. T. Barnes via David W. Menard*

F-100D s/n 56-2965 engages in a flight in clean condition. Notice the long, protruding pitot tube extending under its nose chine. *Courtesy David W. Menard Collection*

This longitudinal cross-section of the D version displays all critical components and subsystems.

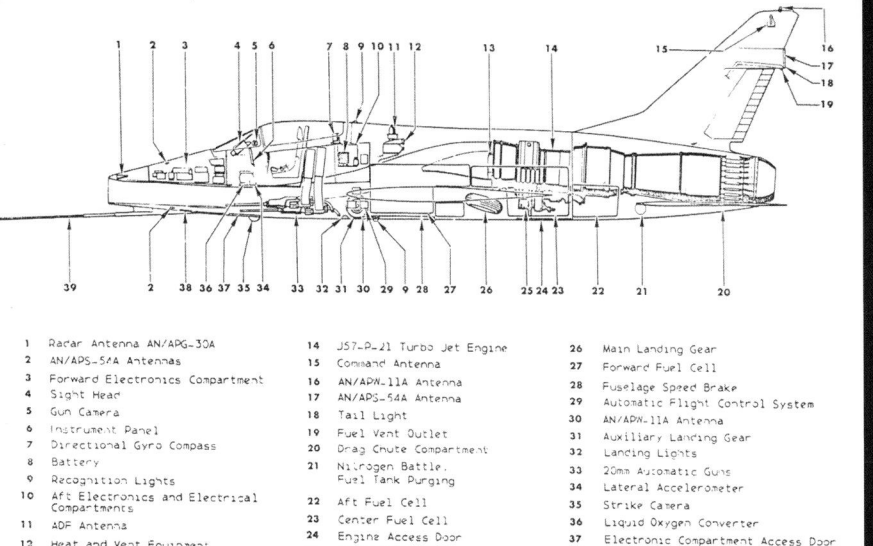

1 Radar Antenna AN/APG-30A
2 AN/APS-54A Antennas
3 Forward Electronics Compartment
4 Sight Head
5 Gun Camera
6 Instrument Panel
7 Directional Gyro Compass
8 Battery
9 Recognition Lights
10 Aft Electronics and Electrical Compartments
11 ADF Antenna
12 Heat and Vent Equipment
13 Engine Accessory Gear Box
14 J57-P-21 Turbo Jet Engine
15 Command Antenna
16 AN/APW-11A Antenna
17 AN/APS-54A Antenna
18 Tail Light
19 Fuel Vent Outlet
20 Drag Chute Compartment
21 Nitrogen Battle, Fuel Tank Purging
22 Aft Fuel Cell
23 Center Fuel Cell
24 Engine Access Door
25 Under Engine Accessory Gear Box
26 Main Landing Gear
27 Forward Fuel Cell
28 Fuselage Speed Brake
29 Automatic Flight Control System
30 AN/APW-11A Antenna
31 Auxiliary Landing Gear
32 Landing Lights
33 20mm Automatic Guns
34 Lateral Accelerometer
35 Strike Camera
36 Liquid Oxygen Converter
37 Electronic Compartment Access Door
38 APX-25 Antenna (IFF)
39 Pitot-Boom

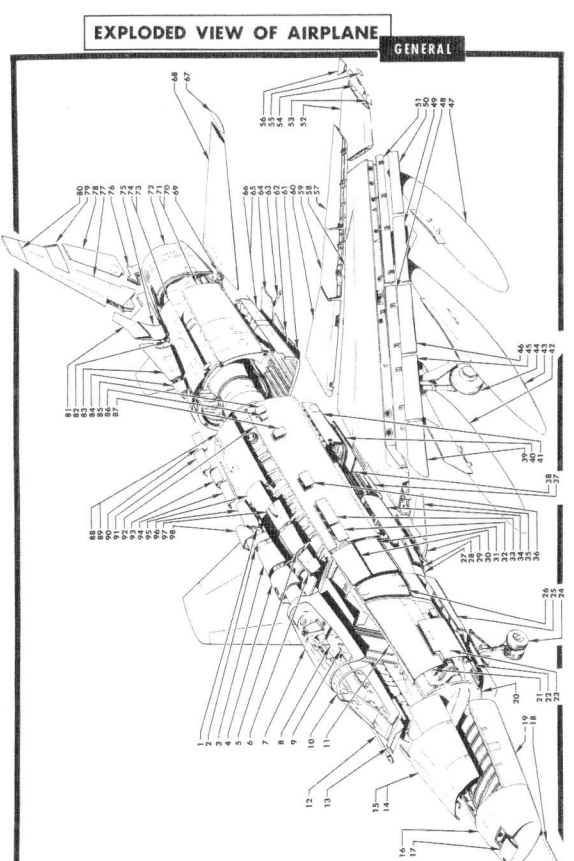

A three-quarter exploded view of the entire F-100D.

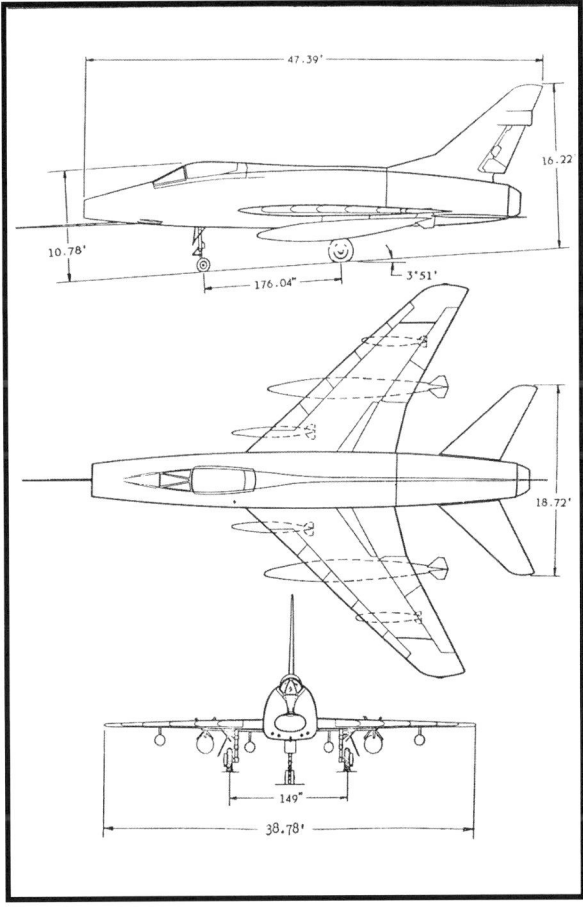

A factory three-view of the F-100 Super Sabre.

F-100D

The F-100D was the most celebrated and widely produced variant of the Super Sabre. It was especially designed for the fighter-bomber role, which it nobly and artfully performed during the Vietnam conflict. Because of its anticipated role as a fighter-bomber, the F-100D embodied an increase in wing and overall tail area, carried an autopilot, had an in-flight refueling system, and a "buddy" system (in which one F-100 could refuel another F-100) for added aerial refueling. The F-100D carried a pair of rather robust 450-gallon external wing tanks with provision to utilize 200-, 275-, and 335-gallon tanks as well. The improvements also added additional weight, thus increasing landing speeds substantially. To help alleviate the weight and speed issues, the F-100D was designed with an additional set of flaps, giving the D-model Super Sabre its cranked-wing trailing edge, the most obvious and distinguishing feature of the type. The air force made provisions to extend its airframe service life from three thousand hours to seven thousand hours.

It is of particular note that during an aerial demonstration by U.S. Air Force Thunderbirds demonstration team, Captain "Tony" McPeak's F-100D came apart during a performance in 1967. The plane's wings folded, gallons of raw fuel burst forth, and the aircraft exploded. McPeak was able to eject safely one or two seconds after the explosion. This singular, spectacular event caused tremendous anxiety both in the air force and at NAA. Engineers devised a temporary external strap as an interim fix until a complete structural modification program was imposed by the U.S. Air Force on 682 F-100Ds.

F-100F

The training and service-accident rates for pilots mastering the idiosyncrasies of the Hun were quite high. It became apparent to the powers that be that a two-seat trainer version of the Super Sabre was urgently needed. The F-100F was designed to those specifications in hopes of significantly reducing the accident rates. It was argued that a few hours of dual time in the trainer would lower the accident rate.

Design studies for a Super Sabre trainer were initiated on 10 May 1954, and on 2 September 1954 North American presented a proposal to the air force for the modification of a single-seat F-100C to trainer status. The air force loaned F-

A factory three-view of the F-100F.

100C s/n 54-1966 to NAA for the impending modifications. The modified plane took flight on 3 August 1956, and on 7 January 1957 NAA rolled out the first production F-100F Super Sabre trainer (Design NA-243). At the end of May 1957, the first squadron at Nellis Air Force Base was equipped with the new Super Sabre trainer. Some 339 F-100Fs were produced, but there was no appreciable reduction in F-100 accidents. The project was not as successful as had been hoped. This variant designed with accident control in mind did not fare any better than the other models. It was not until the onset of the Vietnam conflict that the two-seat F-100F would find its true calling in the guise of the "Wild Weasel" variant.

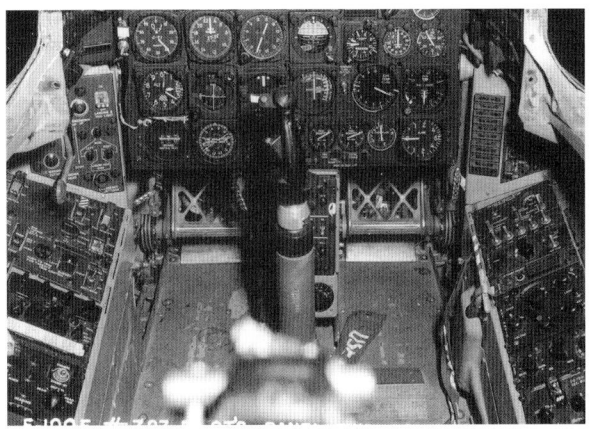

A view of the front cockpit tub of the F-100F showing a full instrument panel, side panels, rudder pedals, and control yoke. *Courtesy Jay Miller Aviation History Collection*

The various Super Sabre models varied significantly in the area of fuel capacity. The F-100A operated on internal fuel cells supplemented by the 275-gallon wing drop tanks. The F-100C fared somewhat better with the incorporation of the wet-wing fuel cells augmented by

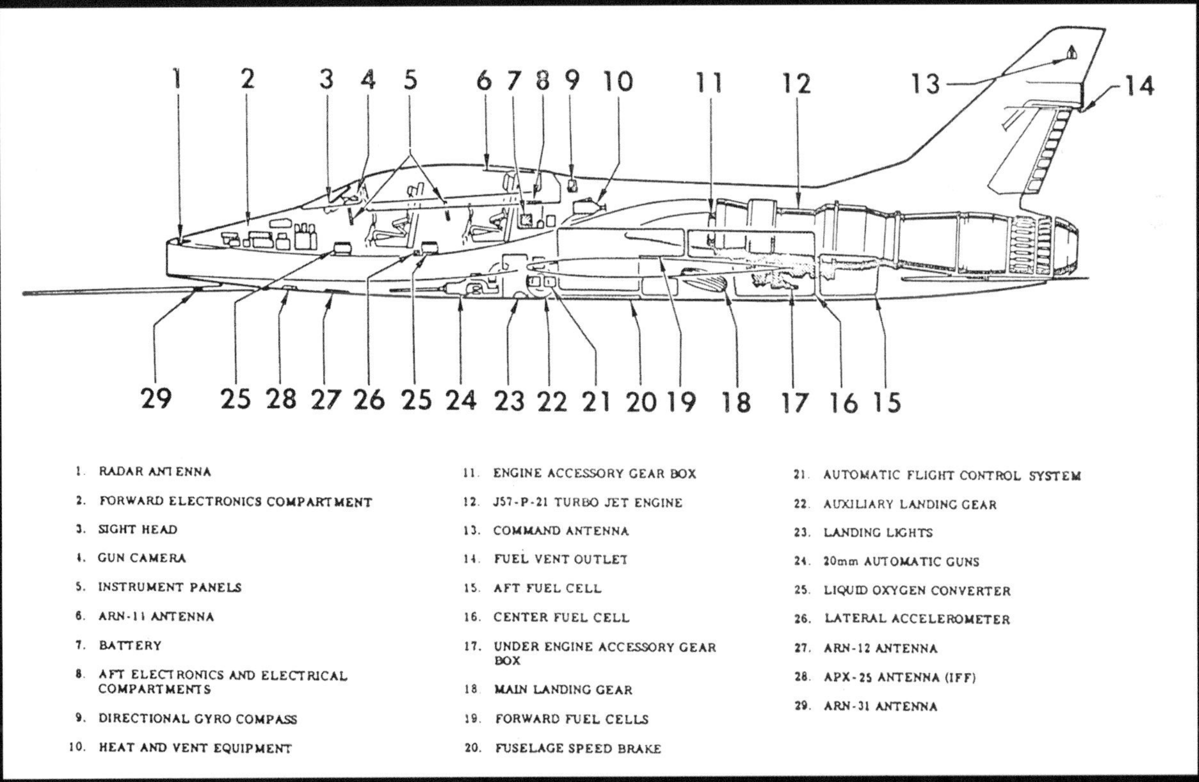

1 2 3 4 5 6 7 8 9 10 11 12 13 14
29 25 28 27 26 25 24 23 22 21 20 19 18 17 16 15
1. RADAR ANTENNA
2. FORWARD ELECTRONICS COMPARTMENT
3. SIGHT HEAD
4. GUN CAMERA
5. INSTRUMENT PANELS
6. ARN-11 ANTENNA
7. BATTERY
8. AFT ELECTRONICS AND ELECTRICAL COMPARTMENTS
9. DIRECTIONAL GYRO COMPASS
10. HEAT AND VENT EQUIPMENT
11. ENGINE ACCESSORY GEAR BOX
12. J57-P-21 TURBO JET ENGINE
13. COMMAND ANTENNA
14. FUEL VENT OUTLET
15. AFT FUEL CELL
16. CENTER FUEL CELL
17. UNDER ENGINE ACCESSORY GEAR BOX
18. MAIN LANDING GEAR
19. FORWARD FUEL CELLS
20. FUSELAGE SPEED BRAKE
21. AUTOMATIC FLIGHT CONTROL SYSTEM
22. AUXILIARY LANDING GEAR
23. LANDING LIGHTS
24. 20mm AUTOMATIC GUNS
25. LIQUID OXYGEN CONVERTER
26. LATERAL ACCELEROMETER
27. ARN-12 ANTENNA
28. APX-25 ANTENNA (IFF)
29. ARN-31 ANTENNA

A cutaway of the F-100F.

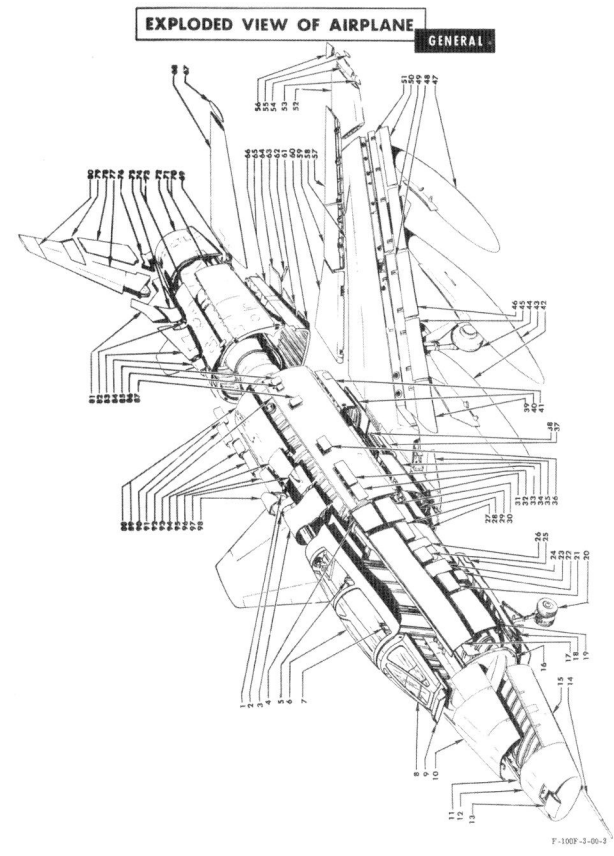

fuselage tanks, two 275-gallon drop tanks, accompanied by in-flight refueling capacity. The F-100D and F variants touted the same capabilities. The F-100A and C utilized three inverters as their prime AC electrical power source, while the F-100D and F versions relied on one engine-driven AC generator with one standby inverter. Engine starts were initiated pneumatically in the A and C variants, while engine starts were actuated by both cartridge and pneumatic sources in the D and F versions. The differences between all four versions were moderate in comparison to other military aircraft contemporary to the Super Sabre.

Left: An exploded view of the F-100F variant.

Below: "Weightless 1" was the name and call sign of the F-100F assigned to the Aeromedical Laboratory at Brooks Air Force Base, Texas, and used to fly parabolic flight patterns for weightless training. Take note of the fully extended air brake. *Courtesy Jay Miller Aviation History Collection*

MAIN DIFFERENCES TABLE
F-100 SERIES

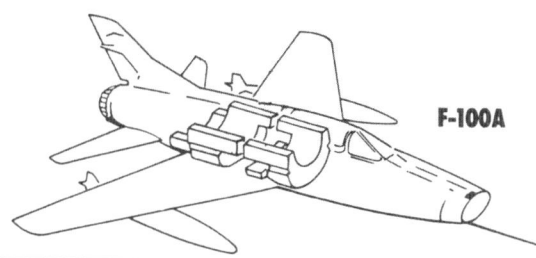

F-100A

ENGINE	J57-21A WITH AFTERBURNER
AC ELECTRICAL POWER SOURCE	THREE INVERTERS
ARMAMENT	FOUR GUNS AND MISSILES
STARTER	PNEUMATIC
DROP TANKS	TWO 275-GALLON
INTERNAL FUEL	FUSELAGE
REFUELING PROVISIONS	GRAVITY TANK FILLING
FLAPS	NO
OXYGEN SYSTEM	GASEOUS, WITH D-2 REGULATOR
AUTOPILOT	NO

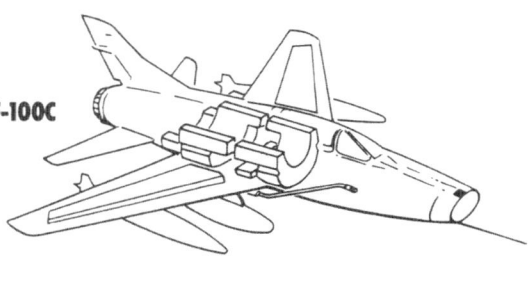

F-100C

ENGINE	J57-21A WITH AFTERBURNER
AC ELECTRICAL POWER SOURCE	THREE INVERTERS
ARMAMENT	FOUR GUNS AND VARIOUS COMBINATIONS OF EXTERNAL LOADS INCLUDING BOMBS, ROCKETS AND MISSILES MOUNTED ON REMOVABLE PYLONS.
STARTER	PNEUMATIC
DROP TANKS	TWO 275-GALLON AND/OR COMBINATION OF 200-GALLON (TWO 335-GALLON ON SOME AIRPLANES)
INTERNAL FUEL	FUSELAGE AND WING
REFUELING PROVISIONS	PRESSURE TYPE (SINGLE-POINT AND AIR REFUELING)
FLAPS	NO
OXYGEN SYSTEM	LIQUID, WITH D-2A REGULATOR
AUTOPILOT	NO

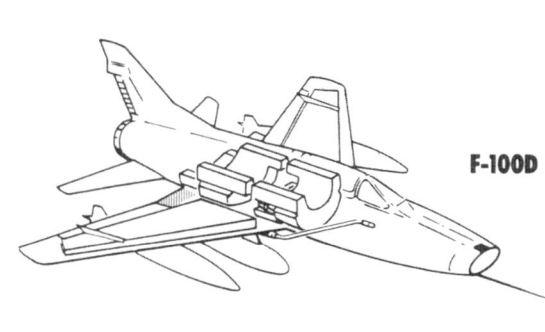

F-100D

ENGINE	J57-21A WITH AFTERBURNER
AC ELECTRICAL POWER SOURCE	ONE ENGINE-DRIVEN AC GENERATOR WITH ONE STAND-BY INVERTER
ARMAMENT	FOUR GUNS AND VARIOUS COMBINATIONS OF EXTERNAL LOADS INCLUDING BOMBS, ROCKETS, AND MISSILES MOUNTED ON FORCE EJECTION PYLONS.
STARTER	CARTRIDGE AND PNEUMATIC
DROP TANKS	TWO 275-GALLON, TWO 450-GALLON OR TWO 335-GALLON AND/OR COMBINATION OF 200-GALLON.
INTERNAL FUEL	FUSELAGE AND WING
REFUELING PROVISIONS	PRESSURE-TYPE (SINGLE-POINT AND AIR REFUELING)
FLAPS	YES
OXYGEN SYSTEM	LIQUID WITH MD-1 REGULATOR
AUTOPILOT	YES

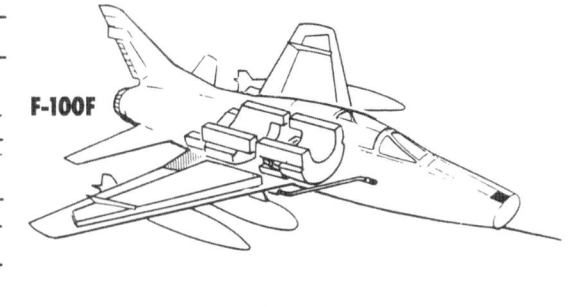

F-100F

ENGINE	J57-21A WITH AFTERBURNER
AC ELECTRICAL POWER SOURCE	ONE ENGINE-DRIVEN AC GENERATOR WITH ONE STAND-BY INVERTER
ARMAMENT	TWO GUNS AND VARIOUS COMBINATIONS OF EXTERNAL LOADS INCLUDING BOMBS, ROCKETS, AND MISSILES MOUNTED ON FORCE EJECTION PYLONS
STARTER	CARTRIDGE AND PNEUMATIC
DROP TANKS	TWO 275-GALLON TWO 450-GALLON OR TWO 335-GALLON AND/OR COMBINATION OF 200-GALLON.
INTERNAL FUEL	FUSELAGE AND WING
REFUELING PROVISIONS	PRESSURE-TYPE (SINGLE-POINT AND AIR REFUELING)
FLAPS	YES
OXYGEN SYSTEM	LIQUID WITH MD-1 REGULATOR
AUTOPILOT	YES

This chart explores the salient differences of all the F-100 models. The most significant is their respective differences in fuel capacity.

A Texas Air National Guard F-100D banks left for the camera aircraft. Notice the powder residue on the 20mm cannon fairings. *Courtesy Jay Miller Aviation History Collection*

CHAPTER 5

WEAPONS SYSTEMS

THE F-100 SUPER SABRE was initially designed as an air superiority fighter. Because of latent deficiencies discovered late in its flight-test performance, its role as a viable fighter was diminished. With the advent of the C and D variants, particularly the D version, the Super Sabre came into its own, not as a dogfighter, but as a potent fighter-bomber.

CANNONS

One instrument of destruction common to all variants was the M39 20mm cannon. Models A through D had two cannons per side of the cockpit. The F variant only carried two cannons, one per side of the pilot's enclosure. The four guns used in models A through D were mounted in the upside-down position and were vented by slats adjacent to them in the fuselage. The muzzles of the guns were positioned in blast slots located in the chin of the Hun. In the single-seat F-100, they could be fired from upper or lower pair, or all together.

The M39 was an advanced version of the T160 gun. Tested in the F-86F Sabre in Korea, the gun was placed into production by General Electric's Pontiac Division around 1953. This weapon was developed from research

An armorer refills the ammunition cans with 20mm rounds on a 478th TFS F-100B circa 1959. *Doug Henderson via Jay Miller Aviation History Collection*

This front underside view denotes the positions and relative arrangement of this Hun's four M39 cannons.
Courtesy Jay Miller Aviation History Collection

based upon the German World War II Mauser MG213C gun, and was based on a totally new and original design incorporating a revolver-type cylinder to fire its shells, significantly increasing its rate of fire. The original German design relied on the use of 30mm ammunition.

Designers at the Illinois Institute of Technology created the M39 gun and initiated some much-needed improvements. By changing the ammunition size from

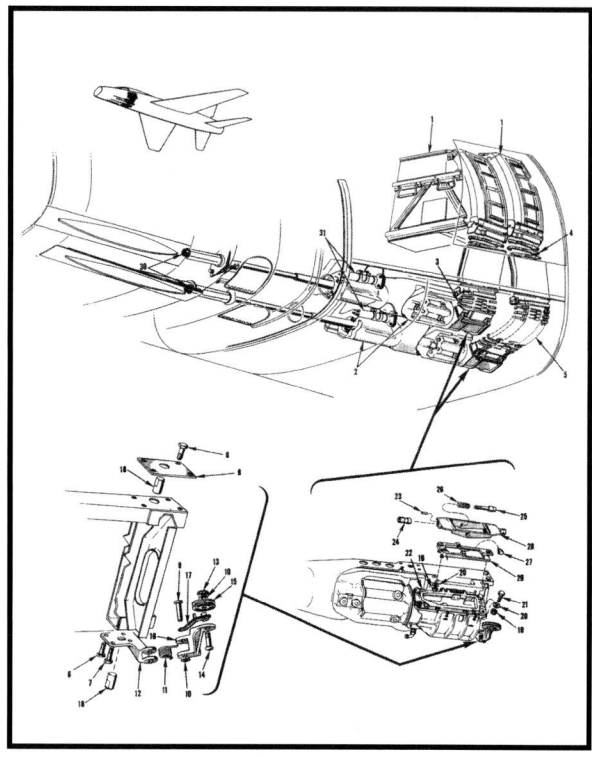

The relative location and inner workings of the M39 cannons are indicated in this drawing. Accompanying the cannons are their respective ammunition canisters.

This group assembly parts list denotes the location of the 20mm cannons and their ammunition boxes. Also notice the inboard pylons used for other ordnance.

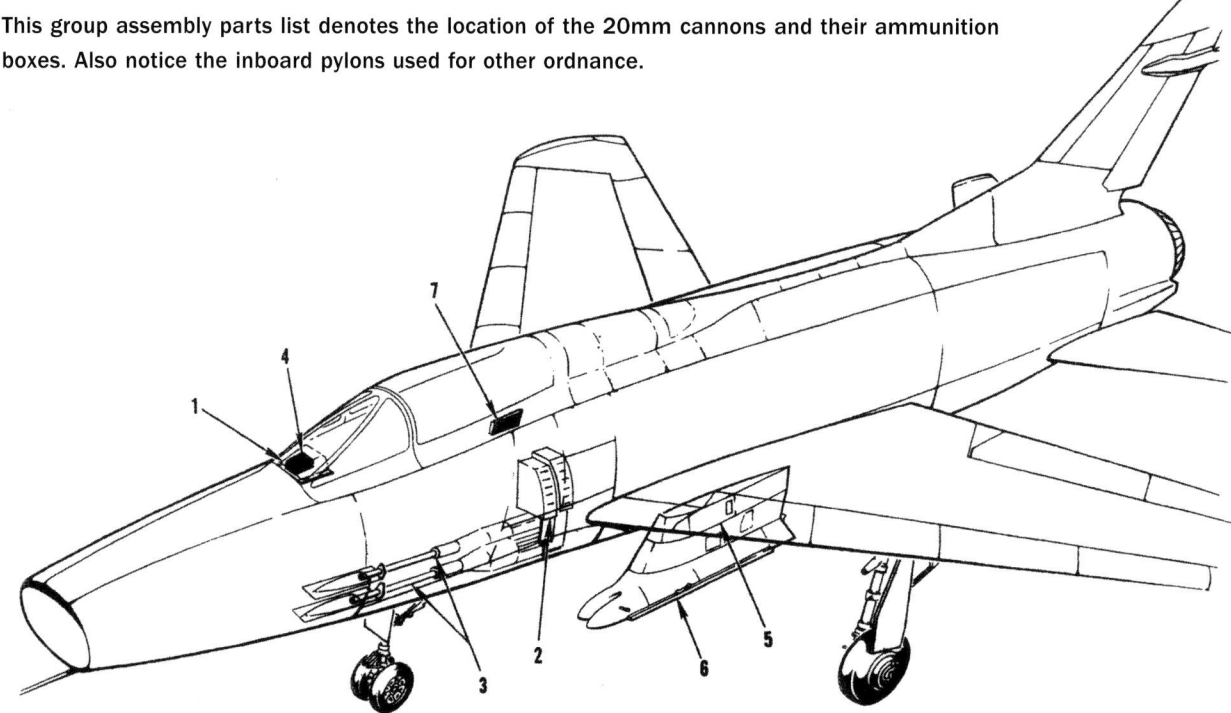

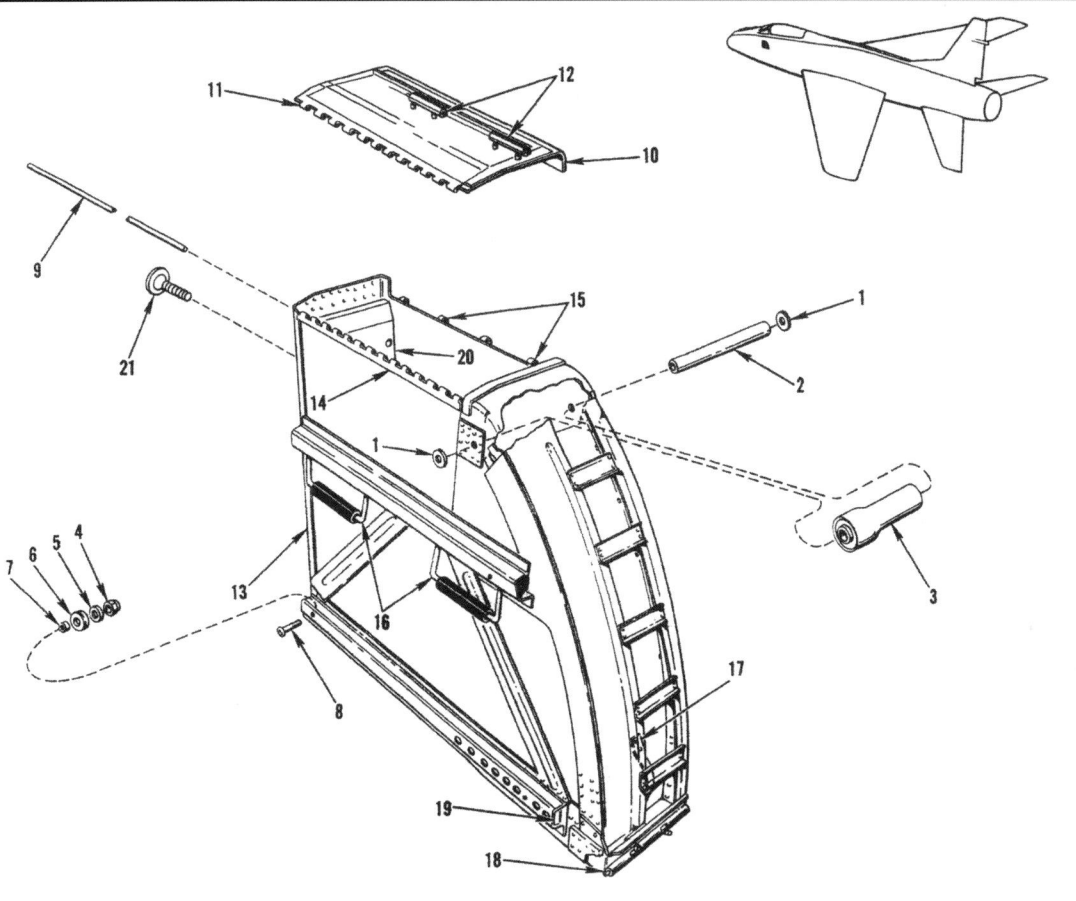

FIGURE & INDEX NUMBER	PART NUMBER	1 2 3 4 5 6 7 NOMENCLATURE	UNITS PER ASSY.	USEABLE ON CODE
312	180-61010-11	BOX ASSY, Ammunition complete LH (192-53074 mod) . . . . (see fig. 304 for breakdown)	Ref	
	180-61010-12	BOX ASSY, Ammunition complete RH (192-53074 mod) . . . . (see fig. 304 for breakdown)	Ref	
-1	AN960D516	. WASHER	2	
-2	180-61019	. SHAFT, M39 gun ammunition box roller	1	
-3	192-61042	. ROLLER ASSY, M39 gun ammunition box	1	
-4	AN310-3	. NUT	2	
-5	2W1-13-12-32	. WASHER, (North American)	2	
-6	180-61036	. ROLLER, Ammunition box track	2	
-7	4B21S3-010	. BUSHING, (North American)	2	
-8	7S13-1032-13	. SCREW, (North American)	2	
-9	AN253-2-1375	. PIN	1	
-10	180-61012-1	. COVER ASSEMBLY, Ammunition box top LH	1	
	180-61012-2	. COVER ASSEMBLY, Ammunition box top RH	1	
-11	180-61012-7	. . HINGE, Half (altered from AN257HC2-1350)	1	
-12	11-8105-3	. . HINGE, Hood instant release (Micro Metal)	2	
-13	180-61011-1	. BOX ASSEMBLY, Ammunition LH	1	
	180-61011-2	. BOX ASSEMBLY, Ammunition RH	1	
-14	180-61011-63	. . HINGE, Half (altered from AN257HC2-1350)	1	
-15	11-7105-3	. . HINGE, Hood instant release (Micro Metal)	2	
-16	180-61013	. . HANDLE ASSEMBLY, Ammunition box	4	
-17	180-61067	. . SPRING, Ammunition box anti-siphon	1	
-18	5-1501AL	. . RELEASE ASSY, Quick LH (Micro Metal) (use 180-61069-1 . . untl exh)	1	
	5-1501AR	. . RELEASE ASSY, Quick RH (Micro Metal) (use 180-61069-2 . . untl exh)	1	
-19	180-61099	. BLOCK, T160 gun ammunition box rail spacer (LH and RH) . . .	1	
-20	192-53061-1	. BALLAST, Ammunition compartment LH	1	
	192-53061-2	. BALLAST, Ammunition compartment RH	1	
-21	SP1561-1032-12	. SCREW, (Shakeproof)	4	

One of the four ammunition canisters needed for the operation of the cannons.

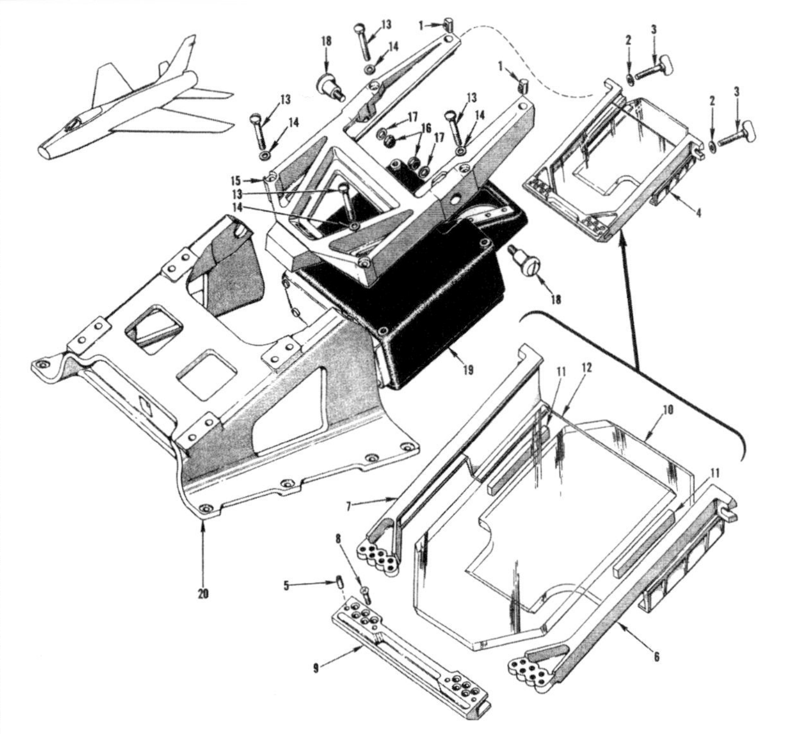

FIGURE & INDEX NUMBER	PART NUMBER	1 2 3 4 5 6 7 NOMENCLATURE	UNITS PER ASSY.	USEABLE ON CODE
303	180-69001-11	SIGHT INSTL, A4A gun-bomb-rocket	NP	
-1	S1452-048	. NUT, (Elastic)	2	
-2	AN960D416	. WASHER	2	
-3	187-69009-15	. LOCKING ASSY, A4A GBR sighthead combining glass holder	2	
-4	192-69013	. HOLDER ASSY, A4A GBR sighthead combining glass	1	
-5	192-69015	. . PIN, A4A GBR sighthead combining glass holder	4	
-6	192-69011-1	. . RETAINER, A4A GBR reflector glass upper LH	1	
-7	192-69011-2	. . RETAINER, A4A GBR reflector glass upper RH	1	
-8	AN507C832R8	. . SCREW	10	
-9	180-69012	. . RETAINER, A4A GBR reflector glass lower	1	
	192-69012	. . GLASS ASSY, A4A GBR gunsight and AN-N9 camera reflector	1	
-10	192-66018	. . . REFLECTOR, AN-N9 camera	1	
-11	192-69014	. . . SPACER, A4A GBR sighthead and AN-N9 camera reflector glass	2	
-12	192-69010	. . . GLASS, A4A GBR reflector	1	
-13	AN500AC416-28	. SCREW	4	
-14	AN960D416	. WASHER	4	
-15	180-69002	. ADAPTER ASSY, A4A GBR sighthead mounting	1	
-16	AN364B624	. . NUT	2	
-17	AN960D616L	. . WASHER	2	
-18	180-69009	. . PIN, A4A GBR adapter supporting	2	
-19	667499	. SIGHTHEAD, GBR type A4A (Sperry) (GFAE) (RDI E201)	1	
-20	180-69003	SUPPORT ASSY, A4A GBR sighthead mounting (see fig. 95)	Ref	

30mm to 20mm, a higher rate of fire could be achieved. Operation of the gun originated when M50-series shells were fed from a belt, accumulating from left to right into a five-chamber, gas-operated revolving cylinder. The revolving cylinder was located at the six o'clock position. Each 20mm casing and round weighed 3.56 ounces, and when fired the projectile left the barrel with a muzzle velocity of 2,850 feet per second. The entire weapon assembly was six feet long and weighed 178 pounds.

With the guns located securely inside the F-100, ammunition was supplied from four magazines, two each side of the cockpit enclosure. The normal limit of ammunition was 200 rounds per magazine, but as much as 275 rounds could be carried if the issue was pressed. The F-100Fs carried only 175 rounds per magazine and incorporated only two magazines per aircraft. The gun barrels on the F-100F vibrated excessively during use, which subjected the aircraft to mild buffeting. Manual charging of the guns was performed on each aircraft before takeoff to eliminate automatic charging in flight from the cockpit.

Above: An assembly diagram for the A-4 gunsight, bomb, and rocket sign installation.

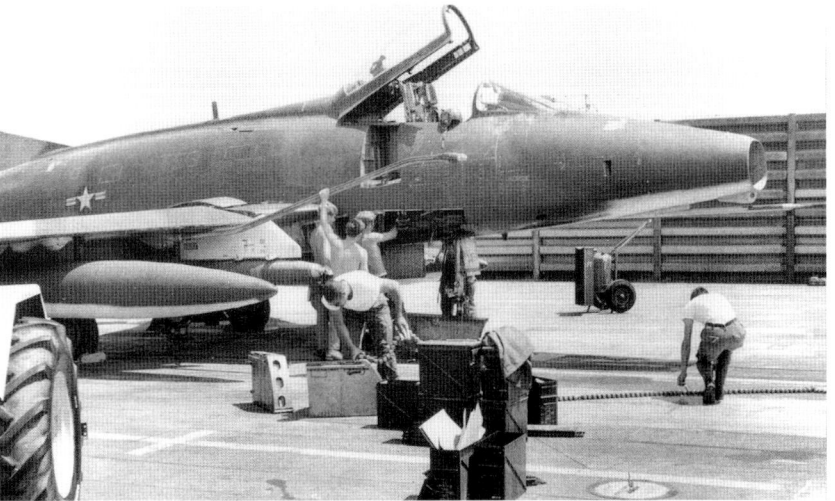

Right: Armorers load an F-100D in South Vietnam. Notice the individual ammunition boxes in the foreground along with the exposed M39 cannon in the F-100D. *T/Sgt. Norman E. Taylor*

Spent ammunition casings were ejected via tubes flush with the lower fuselage. They were expelled with sufficient force as to inhibit their contact with the aircraft. Expended ammunition links were retained in a separate compartment next to the guns for later reprocessing and reuse.

The gases expelled from the detonation of each shell were vented from the gun compartment by a purging system. This particular system drew air from the main air intake duct via automatic doors to expel the accumulating gases. This system was activated when the pilot squeezed the trigger to its first detent position. Air was accepted through this system for an additional five seconds after firing the guns ceased. In the event of a purge door failing to open, a microswitch disabled current flowing of the gun firing circuits.

When firing of the guns was performed on the ground, all hatches for the guns and ammunition bays were removed for adequate ventilation to occur. Venting of the gun bay was of paramount importance, especially during prolonged gun bursts. Expended shell gases could build up quickly, causing an explosion if vented rapidly.

Ford Aerospace Tiger Claws improved on the basic M39 cannon design by increasing its rate of fire to 2,300 rounds per minute and reducing the weight by 20 percent. The endurance life of the gun was significantly increased to 10,000 rounds. The M39 eventually lost favor with the air force in lieu of the M61 Vulcan "Gatling gun," which was standard equipment on the next generation of U.S. combat aircraft.

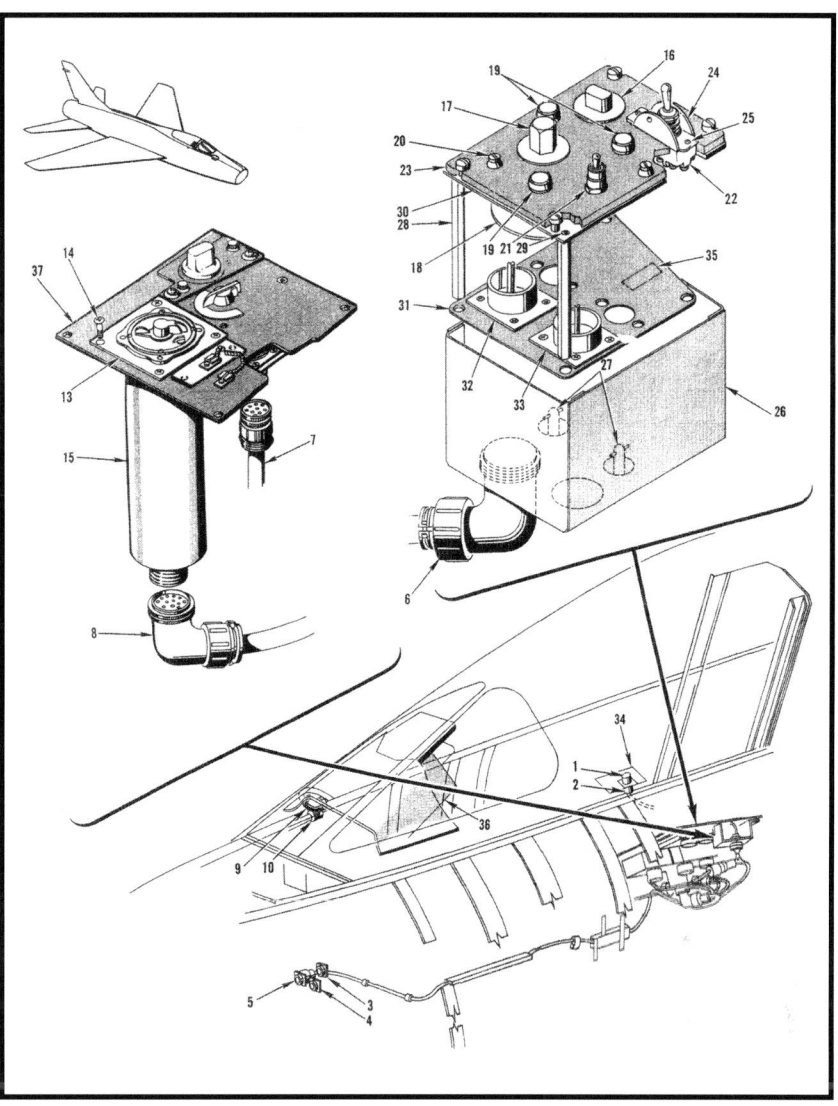

A diagram and breakdown of the AN/APG 30 radar equipment used on the F-100A and C variants.

F-100A AND C WEAPONS

The internal armament for both F-100A and C variants consisted of four Pontiac M39E 20mm cannons located in the lower fuselage. Aiming of the guns was aided through the use of an A4 gun sight. Provisions were made, especially on the C version, for the use of six underwing hard points carrying up to 6,000 pounds of munitions or fuel. This was 1,500 pounds less than what the F-100D could muster. Provisions were also made to incorporate the use of chemical tanks, missiles, or jettisonable pylons under the wings. The A4 sight could accommodate weapons use in gun, bomb, and rocket sighting and was coupled with a radar ranging system for sighting enhancement.

A4 SIGHT: The type A4 gyro computing sight automatically computed lead distance for gunnery and bombing functions. This sight computation was fully

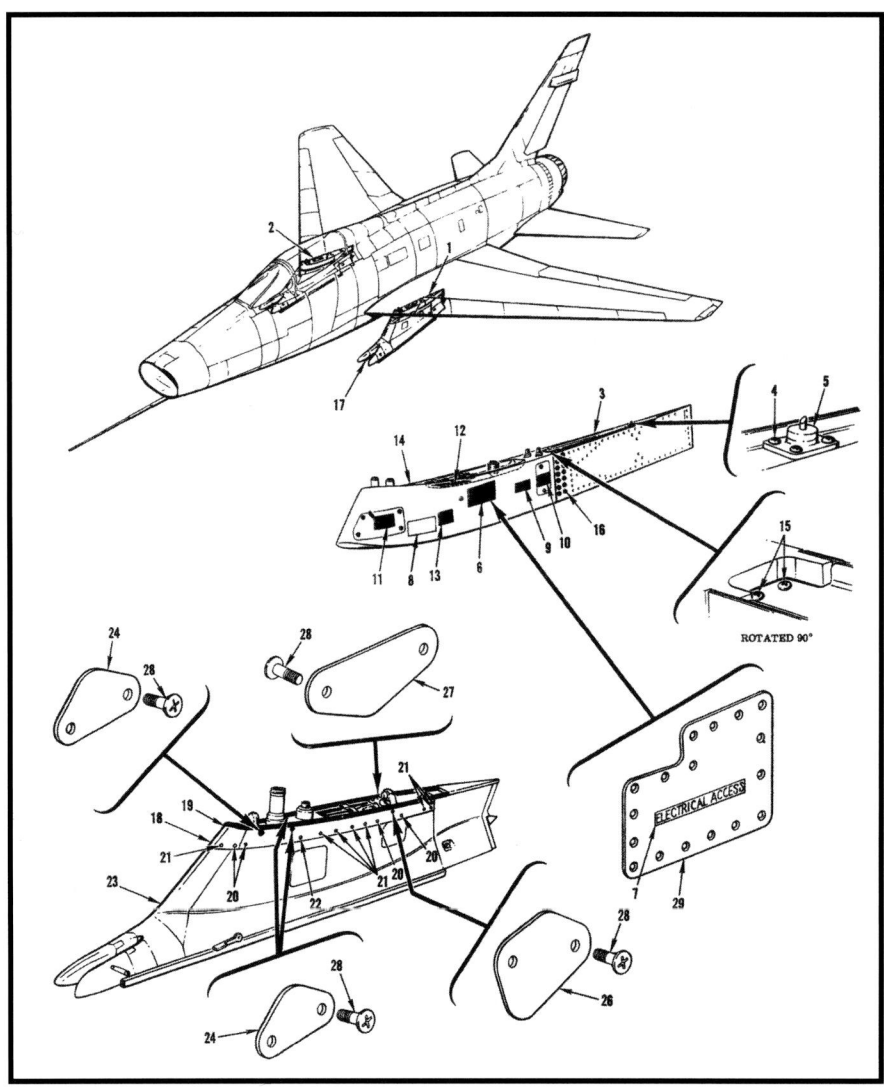

This pylon and adapter were utilized especially when employing the use of AIM-9B Sidewinder air-to-air missiles.

automatic. Its only requirement was for the pilot to keep the reticle's center pipper (a spot of light projected by the plane's computing gun sight) focused and tracking the target smoothly. The reticle image was projected on a reflector glass aft of the windshield. Range data was supplied by the radar ranging system supplemented by a standard manual range control. When the A4 gun sight was pressed into service as a bombsight, the sighting system was calibrated to compute automatically the lead of the target between distances ranging from 600 to 6,000 feet. The line of sight was, in fact, depressed additionally in order for the flight path to intersect the proper bomb release point. Bombs could be released several ways, the first of which, automatic release, could be achieved by the use of an accelerator mechanism located within the gun sight or manually.

SIGHT RANGING RADAR: An AN/ASE-17 radar system supplied and fed range data to the A4 gun sight. The radar's search range varied from 2,000 to 9,000 feet. The radar system automatically locked on and tracked targets lying within these ranges. A light on the A4 gun sight became activated when a target was acquired. The sight reticle lit up brilliantly during target lock-on. A manual range control supplemented the radar sight and was used often during the event of radar ranging failure. Manual ranging was greatly encouraged during target acquisition below 6,000 feet due to terrain ground-effect clutter.

MANUAL RANGING CONTROL: A twist control located on the throttle grip allowed range data to be supplemented manually to the sight system. This system was used when range radar was ineffective due to inordinate interference from ground effects. Manual ranging was operated in 1,500-foot segments, and this span was effective over a range of 1,200 and 2,700 feet. Range data was displayed on the sight range dial. The sight reticle diameter was controlled by the manual operation of the throttle grip. The clockwise rotation of the throttle grip reduced range. Likewise, counter-clockwise rotation increased range. The throttle twist grip was spring-loaded to the full counter-clockwise position. This was the correct position for full automatic operation of the radar ranging equipment.

TRIGGER: The trigger located on the control yoke grip was responsible for activating the firing of the gun and missiles, and initiated the gun-bay purge system and gun camera. Missiles were fired with the trigger pressed to the second detent only when the trigger safety switch was at the missile camera position, along with the other properly orientated switches.

BOMBING EQUIPMENT: The F-100 had two ordnance stations located inboard of the drop tank stations that were equipped with forced-ejection type of pylons. The pilot had the option of the manual or automatic release of munitions, or they could be jettisoned electronically.

EJECTOR TYPE OF PYLON: There were essentially two methods of pylons or munitions fastening techniques employed on the Super Sabre. The first was the conventional bomb rack, and the second was the ejector-type pylon. The type of ordnance carried usually dictated what type of release method was to be used. There were two electronically ignited charges located in the pylon that jettisoned the load. The ejector-type pylon utilized two separate and complete ignition circuits: one primary, and the other an emergency circuit. When the primary charge was ignited, the force and pressure from its ignition detonated the emergency circuit as well, insuring total release of the weapon. Conversely, if the primary circuit failed, the emergency circuit was activated, which in turn set off the failed charges. When iron bombs or napalm were carried, a bypass valve was held open, allowing most of the activated ejection pressure to be dumped overboard the aircraft, so the actual release of the munitions closely approximated a free-fall type of trajectory. As a point of interest, the pylons could be forcibly ejected from the wing only when the emergency jettison circuit was activated.

BOMB RELEASE PROCEDURE USING A4 SIGHT: The following procedure is taken from the official F-100A Flight Manual. Bomb release was achieved when adhering to the following processes:

- Turn bomb release mode selector switch to sight and radar to allow a five- to fifteen-minute warm-up period for the sight. Check sight mechanical caging lever at cage.
- Move sight filament selector switch to pri (primary). If primary filament is inoperative, move switch to sec (secondary).
- Adjust sight dimmer rheostat to desired reticle image brilliance.
- Move sight mechanical caging lever to uncage.
- Position armament selector switch for load carrier.
- Turn sight function selector lever to bomb.
- Turn bomb release mode selector switch to dive or manual.
- After sighting target, and before starting approach, set bomb-arming switch at nose and tail or tail only.
- Adjust bomb-target wind control toward upwind or downwind, depending on known or estimated wind velocity at the target.
- Make approach to target that will give desired dive angle during bombing run.
- Press sight electrical caging button to stabilize reticle image before pushing over into dive.
- Place reticle image pipper on target.
- After dive is established, keep pipper on target and release electrical caging button. If bomb release mode selector switch is at dive, press bomb button at this time.
- If release is manual, press bomb button when sight aiming circle and pipper go out.

MISSILE SYSTEM: The F-100 series of aircraft could employ two missile systems. They were the AIM-9B Sidewinder air-to-air and AGM-12B Bullpup air-to-ground missile systems.

AIM-9B SYSTEM (SIDEWINDER): Two AIM-9B (GAR-8) Sidewinder missiles could be deployed on a type IXA pylon located at each inboard wing station. This type of missile was of the air-to-air type guided by a passive infrared homing system and proved highly successful in battle. The missile was nine feet long, with a slender, constant five-inch-diameter cross-section. It weighed approximately 155 pounds and was constructed in four major sections. Nose to tail, the guidance and control was the first followed by the warhead, fuse, and rocket motor. All power was supplied to the missile from the aircraft while still attached. A gas-driven generator supplied electrical power to all guidance and control while the missile was in flight. The propellant used to power the AIM-9B was slow-burning chemical grain. The motor section also held the stabilizing fins responsible for the missile directional control. The warhead was detonated by direct contact or by influence fuse. Guidance was augmented by the use of four movable fin gyros that enhanced directional control and maneuverability. These devices were coined as rollerons and

F-100D s/n 55-2881 awaits her next drone target mission. *Courtesy Jay Miller Aviation History Collection*

helped limit roll of the missile. The Sidewinder was aimed by the A4 gun sight incorporating a fixed reticle. If the pilot heard a consistent tone generated from the missile in his headset, the missile was locked on target.

MISSILE SYSTEM CONTROLS AND INDICATORS: The missile control systems responsible for the AIM-9B missile functions are as follows:
- Missile master switch: initiated the entire power system for proper missile function.
- Station bypass switch: simply bypassed a malfunctioning missile for the next.
- Ready signal volume control: a rheostat that provided volume control from audio signals emitted from the missile.
- Safe launch button: provided for the simultaneous salvo launch of unarmed missiles.
- Missile indicator lights: informed the pilot that the missiles were ready for launch.
- Trigger safety switch: insured a higher degree of safety against misfire of missiles.
- Trigger: firing switch.
- Ground fire switch.
- External load emergency jettison button: provided safe jettisoning of missiles and munitions during an emergency.

AGM-12B MISSILE SYSTEM (BULLPUP): The AGM-12B (GAM-83A) Bullpup was an air-to-surface pilot-guided missile carried on a type XA launcher positioned at both inboard wing stations. It was usually launched between 250 knots indicated airspeed and maximum allowable air speed. The missile weighed 570 pounds, was 10.5 feet long, and possessed a rather robust cross-

A well-worn combat veteran F-100D of the 307th TFS, 31st TFW, on temporary duty at Bien Hoa Air Base, Republic of Vietnam, in the late fall of 1965 carries two medium-blue bands on her fin. A "BB stacker" is driving his MJ1 "Jammer" with a 750-pound bomb to another Hun for loading. *Courtesy Jay Miller Aviation History Collection*

section measuring 1 foot in diameter. The warhead was located at midsection of the missile structure and was either of the high-explosive or fragmentation type. The front portion of the missile housed the guidance system, a battery, and a bomb-fuse initiator. A compressed-air bottle was also situated in the nose section, along with two pairs of movable control fins. These served as canards and were activated and controlled by air pressure from the bottle through pneumatic valves. The aft section housed either a liquid or solid propellant and the appropriate rocket motor. The rocket motor, upon ignition, would perform for approximately two seconds, while the missile deployed flares to aid in the missile's tracking once fired.

The aft portion of the missile also included four guidance fins, which were highly cambered at the tip to impart a 500-degree-per-second roll rate to the missile after its launch. As a point of note, this missile produced 10,500 pounds of thrust upon ignition.

AGM-12B MISSILE SYSTEM CONTROL AND INDICATORS:

The trigger and trigger-safety switch: a multi-function apparatus used for operation of the 20mm cannon, munitions release, and the firing of missiles.

Missile-control switch: could be operated in three separate modes: off, STBY (standby), and ready. When the switch was located in the off position, power was disabled to the missile firing system. In standby mode, the system was warming up; and, in ready position, the circuit was fully energized, ready for missile release.

Missile selector switch: determined which of the missiles would be fired or safe-launched.

Missile launch mode switch: determined if the missile would be guided to its target or fly unguided as a ballistic rocket.

Missile controller: a self-centering miniature control stick. Guidance commands were initiated when the controller was displaced off center. This mechanism dwelled in the areas marked down, up, L (left), and R (right). Any position in between these designated areas initiated simultaneously-sent signals from the controller to the horizontal and vertical directional guide vanes. This was performed in conjunction with the line of sight on the target. Data on the movement of the controller and its subsequent transmissions were emitted through the F-100's antenna to four receiver antennas—one per stabilizing fin—on the missile. The transmitter accomplished this through the provision of proportional responses to the duration and magnitude of controller deflection. These signal pulses were relayed to the missile where they were decoded to the missile reference axis by the use of a roll-referenced gyro. The impulses through the use of the roll-referenced gyro initiated the proper deflection of the forward canards, enhancing directional stability. The mechanical movement of the canards was facilitated by pneumatic pressure generated by an air bottle located in the nose of the vehicle and operated in conjunction with servo units powered by this pneumatic pressure.

Missile indicator lights: Two to four placard-type indicator lights were employed with the use of the AGM-12B missile system. The missile indicator lights only activated when the aircraft was airborne and the unlaunched missiles were at the selected station in

An armorer is getting ready to install the fuse into a 500-pound bomb under a 478th TFS F-100D. *Doug Henderson via Jay Miller Aviation History Collection*

The F-102A afterburner nozzle eyelids show up well in this view of a QF-100D, a drone version of the F-100D. *Courtesy Jay Miller Aviation History Collection*

conjunction with the following switch settings:
- Trigger safety switch at missile camera.
- Missile selector switch at L or R.
- Missile launch mode switch at guide or unguided.
- Missile control switch at ready.

After missile discharge, whether in controlled or safe-launch mode, the indicator lights remained on, with one of the following occurring: the trigger safety switch, missile selection switch, or missile control switch was repositioned.

ARMAMENT EQUIPMENT FOR F-100D AND F-100F

Most F-100Ds were manufactured with provisions for seven pylons, all of which carried ordnance. In theory, the F-100D variant could embrace a total load consisting of four 1,000-pound stores (fuel tanks, etc.), eight 750-pound bombs, and ten 500-pound bombs, which required the use of triple ejector racks. During operations, even in combat, the F-100 rarely carried more than one store per pylon, and in most applications, the intermediate pylon was utilized for the incorporation of auxiliary fuel tanks. Four of the hard points embedded in the wings were specifically used in the hauling of ordnance, such as bombs, rockets, or napalm. In its other role as free-world defender and nuclear fighter-bomber, the Hun was cleared to carry the MK7, B28, B43, B57, and B61 nuclear weapons.

These Huns embraced a fairly new bombing technique called low-altitude bombing system (LABS), where the aircraft would accelerate to high speeds at tree-top level, which upon target acquisition would initiate an immediate pull-up, releasing the ordnance (nuclear or conventional) to follow its own ballistic trajectory to the target.

Some F-100Ds and F-100Cs were modified to carry the AGM-12 Bullpup, while others flew with AIM-9B Sidewinders. Because the F-100F wing was configured to that of the F-100D, both models retained the same ordnance capacity.

The F-100F, in its Wild Weasel configuration, could be easily distinguished from other F-model Super Sabres, or any other F-100 for that matter, by its Vector IV radar homing and warning (RHAW) system, sporting a pair of antennas, each of which faced outwardly at a 45-degree angle under the front intake and a pair situated on the trailing edge of the vertical fin. The IR-133 threat-analysis system utilized three flush antennas. The WR-300 launch warning receiver (LWR) used two smaller antennas located in front of the nose-wheel door. The Vector IV system embodied the use of a three-inch cathode-ray tube (CRT) display found in both front and rear cockpit enclosures, while the LWR used a simple red launch indicator.

The missile of choice for the Wild Weasel was the AGM-45 radar-homing seeker commonly known as the Shrike. It was highly effective and started the lineage of what is now known as the anti-radiation missiles. It

This Nellis F-100F is carrying four cans of napalm for a firepower demonstration. *Courtesy Jay Miller Aviation History Collection*

Two F-100Ds of the 110th TFS, Missouri Air National Guard, peel off to make a gunnery range pass. *Courtesy Jay Miller Aviation History Collection*

carried a 145-pound fragmentation warhead and ruined the day of many North Vietnamese surface-to-air missile (SAM) operators.

A4 GUN SIGHT: The gun sight on the F-100D and F models was the same one used in the F-100A and C variants, with the exception that some aircraft provisions were made to incorporate the use of LABS, a type of ordnance delivery. This was accomplished by modifying the sight reticle so the light would turn off during the caging cycle of the LABS yaw-run gyro and remain out until gyro caging was completed.

SIGHT RANGING RADAR: The AN/APG-30A radar ranging system was more advanced than the system in the F-100A and C but incorporated the AN/ASG-17 fire-control radar system from the A and C variants as a subsystem in this unit. It improved sight range from 700 to 2,000 feet to a range of 900 to 9,000 feet. Manual range control was to be initiated on targets below 6,000 feet as advised for the A and C variants.

GUNNERY ACQUISITION: The later-model F-100s utilized the same system and techniques employed by the F-100A and C variants.

ARMAMENT SELECTION: Armament selection was achieved through the use of the armament selection switch. This rotary device, powered by the secondary bus, determined the order of external load release when the bomb button was used. Regardless of what release method was used, the selection switch determined the order and sequence of munitions departure.

The 275- and 335-gallon drop tanks and pylons carried by the F-100D and F models were released through solenoid activation and would free fall from the aircraft.

A "Blue Boy" inert special weapon is on display next to a 428th TFS F-100D that could carry it under her left wing. *Doug Henderson via Jay Miller Aviation History Collection*

A Nellis-marked F-100D with six rocket pods taxis for take off to head for the range. *Courtesy Jay Miller Aviation History Collection*

BOMB RELEASE – A4 SIGHT: The primary bomb release for the F-100D and F was similar to the system in the A and C variants, except with the modified M1 bombing system installed in some F-100F aircraft and MA2 low-altitude and AN/AJB low-altitude bombing systems.

M1 BOMBING SYSTEM: The M1 bombing system was used along with the normal bomb-release system incorporating the A4 gun sights (sight reticle caged) in order to aid the pilot during automatic release of bomb-tossing operations. The system was empowered by the tertiary bus and by the main three-phase AC bus. The M1 control panel was used to supply target and ballistics information to the computer via the pilot. The M1 bombing system comprised the following control elements:
Target pressure selector switch: oriented the M1 system to the correct prevailing barometric pressure over the target.
• Gross weight selector switch: this unit set into the system the gross weight of the aircraft flying over the target.
• Ballistics selector switch: accumulated the M1 system to all ballistic data necessary for proper ordnance delivery.
• Wind selector switch: prepared the M1 system to adjust to prevailing wind conditions over the target and was calibrated to as high as 80 knots of either head wind or tail wind.

• Selector switch: used to set the system to the type of bomb function to be used. The initial settings were T (toss bomb), R (radar), S (stand-by), D (direct), and off.
• Cage-uncage switch: located on the M1 control panel, it was used to cage or uncage the M1 gyro. M1 indicator light: lit up during timed or normal release.

MA2 LOW-ALTITUDE BOMBING SYSTEM (LABS): The MA2 low-altitude bombing system was an electro-mechanical-powered system operated in conjunction with the A4 gun sight reticle to provide the most accurate release point for bomb tossing. This system provided the necessary flight maneuver information to initiate accurate bombing. The A4 sight reticle was electrically caged to facilitate this type of bomb release.

ACCELEROMETER: The accelerometer was the device that provided pitch acceleration information to the MA2 system for proper bomb release at altitude.

BOMB RELEASE MODE SELECTOR SWITCH: This was a device to aid the pilot in the release of ordnance.

TIME REFERENCE POINT (TRP) TIMER: The TRP timer sequenced the operation of certain units to be timed in the bombing system.

LABS VERTICAL GYRO CAGING SWITCH: This unit enacted the motion of the LABS vertical gyro to the vertical position. This occurred when the LABS vertical gyro switch was moved to the cage position, which in turn extinguished the sight reticle light when the bomb-release mode was at LABS or LABS altitude.

Conversely, when the switch was moved to uncage, the LABS vertical gyro uncaged and the system became operable. This action ensured that all accurate vertical reference data was transferred to the dive-and-roll indicator.

LABS DIVE-AND-ROLL INDICATOR: This mechanism was a dual movement, zero-centered unit. What this instrument transmitted to the pilot was the axis altitude the aircraft was flying. The vertical dial indicated roll altitude when, in fact, the vertical gyro was uncaged and the yaw-roll gyro was electrically caged. It also indicated yaw-roll altitude when the yaw-roll gyro was totally uncaged. The horizontal pointer in turn displayed aircraft pitch altitude when the vertical gyro was uncaged. During this event, the yaw-roll gyro was also electrically caged. This instrument was activated when the bomb release selector switch was positioned at LABS.

LABS RELEASE INDICATOR LIGHT: This light simply indicated when bomb release occurred during a LABS maneuver.

AN/AJB LOW-ALTITUDE BOMBING SYSTEM (LABS): This LABS unit operated in conjunction with the A4 gun sight reticle during toss-bombing operations. This particular unit was featured in F-100D-20 through F-100D-30, and F-100D-45. Later F-100Ds employed an AN/AJB-1B LABS, while F-100Fs aircraft carried an AN/AJB-5A LABS.

BOMB RELEASE MODE SELECTOR SWITCH: This switch, when positioned at LABS or LABS ACT (air combat tactics), engaged the system and rendered it operable when the desired release angle was selected. If the acceptable LABS angle was excluded, bomb release would not occur.

LABS VERTICAL GYRO CAGING BUTTON: When engaged on the throttle, the LABS vertical gyro was erected vertically when the bomb release switch was placed on LABS, or LABS ACT. It took approximately thirteen seconds to energize fully. After the caging cycle was completed, the gyro became operable, thus ensuring the transfer of accurate vertical reference data to the dive-and-roll indicator. All other controls, like the time reference point (TRP) timer, LABS yaw-roll gyro check button, LABS dive-and-roll indicator, and LABS release indicator light, functioned in the same way as the previously mentioned controls for the MA2 system.

LOW-ALTITUDE DROGUE DELIVERY SYSTEM (LADDS) LOAD: This electro-mechanical device was employed in unison with the A4 gun sight. The system released munitions with a drouge chute attached for slower delivery and in turn determined weapons delivery in terms of time rather than aircraft pitch angle. Controls for LADDS were similar to the LABS system. They included the bomb-release mode selector switch, TRP timer, and the LADDS release timer.

MISSILE CONTROL: Both the F-100D- and F-group aircraft had provisions to utilize the AIM-9B Sidewinder missile. The controls employed in the earlier models were essentially the same in these units. The AGM-12B Bullpup missile was also employed on the F-100D and F models, though more commonly employed in the D version.

This 39th Air Division F-100B was on static display at Misawa Air Base, Japan, circa 1960. *Courtesy David W. Menard*

An F-100F of the Royal Danish Air Force makes a low pass over a lighthouse. *Courtesy Jay Miller Aviation History Collection*

CHAPTER SIX

OPERATORS WORLDWIDE

THE F-100, BEING THE QUINTESSENTIAL aircraft in the U.S. inventory, was also quite popular as a foreign export as well. The F-100 was used by four foreign countries: Denmark, Turkey, Taiwan, and France.

DENMARK
The Danes showed keen interest in the Super Sabre and made efforts to acquire three factory-fresh F-100Fs and seventeen F-100Ds that were siphoned from U.S. inventory. They received seven more F-100Fs and thirty-one F-100Ds in 1961, bringing Denmark's totals to ten F-100Fs and 48 F-100Ds.

These Super Sabres were operated by Eskadrille (ESK) 725, based at Karup, and ESK 727 and 730. Both of these units were stationed by Skrydstrup, located on the Central Jutland Peninsula. These examples replaced aging Republic F-84G fighter-bombers. The three operational units formed the Flyvertaktisk Kommando, which was equivalent to the U.S. Tactical Air Command.

It was not a surprise at that time that F-100s everywhere embraced a terrible safety record. The Danes also experienced these problems to some extent. Eight of the ten F-100Fs were soon lost to crashes as well as twenty-seven of the forty-eight F-100Ds. The first two years of operation, 1962 and 1963, were considered the worst when five of the D models were lost. By 1968, a third of the remaining fleet was lost due to its high accident rate.

By this time, all three of the squadrons were severely under strength. An active squadron required at least

A Royal Danish Air Force F-100F flies formation with a restored P-51D over a U.K. air show. *G. Pennick via David W. Menard*

Two Royal Danish Air Force F-100Ds, s/n 55-2776 and s/n 55-2779, on final approach to RAF base Wethersfield, United Kingdom. *G. Pennick via David W. Menard*

twenty aircraft and a few held for reserves. By September 1970, ESK 725 transferred its remaining F-100s to ESK 727 and 730. ESK 725 was re-equipped with SAAB Draaken fighters. Both ESK 727 and 730 continued to operate the Hun until the early 1980s.

In 1974, the Det Kongelige Danske Flyvevaben (DKDF or Royal Danish Air Force) formed the Operational Conversion Unit (OCU) slated to teach Danish pilots how to fly the Hun. The Danes acquired fourteen F-100Fs from the military aircraft storage

A Royal Danish Air Force F-100D completes its landing roll with its drogue chute deployed. *G. Pennick via Jay Miller Aviation History Collection*

The 401st TFW transferred their F-100Ds to the Turkish Air Force when they transitioned to the McDonnell F-4D Phantom IIs. *Courtesy Jay Miller Aviation History Collection*

disposal center located at Davis-Monthan Air Force Base, Arizona. Eight additional F-100Fs were obtained from inventories in the U.S. Air National Guard. They were slightly modified to Danish specifications and were redesignated TF-100Fs.

From 1974 to 1975, the fleet of F-100s were accident free. The following year, 1976, was not kind to the Danish Super Sabres due to several F-100D and F-100F accidents. After a protracted grounding of all aircraft, service was re-energized for another accident-free two years.

It was during this time that Danish military authorities were in the process of re-equipping all existing squadrons with the new General Dynamics F-16 fighter. By 1985, three F-100s remained in Denmark, two of which took up residency at the Gate of Skrydstrup and the third (s/n 56-3927) resided in a Danish museum.

TURKEY

The Turk Hava Kuvvetleri (THK) (Turkish Air Force) acquired eighty-seven Huns in the late 1950s, encompassing a mixture of the C, D, and F models. After the acquisition process, published reports revealed Turkey had received 206 aircraft, some of which had originated from U.S. Air Force surplus inventory and had come from the Danes.

The Super Sabres obtained at the time were operated by at least five THK filo. (A filo in Turkey was similar to a U.S. Air Force squadron.) Filo 111, located at Eskisehir, operated in conjunction to Filos 131 and 132, located at Konya, and Filos 171 and 172 operated from Erhac, Malatya.

TAIWAN

The Chinese Nationalist Air Force (CNAF) of Taiwan also operated the F-100 in large numbers. The first

F-100F s/n 56-3988 of the Republic of China Air Force (ROCAF) on Taiwan prepares to land. *ROCAF via David W. Menard*

aircraft delivered to the CNAF were F-100Fs. Upon their arrival in 1959, a batch delivery of fifteen F-100As arrived, further supplemented by sixty-five more examples by 1960. By late 1961, four RF-100As (Slick Chicks) arrived to bolster reconnaissance abilities for the CNAF.

In subsequent decades, initial deliveries peaked at an additional thirty-eight A models. The CNAF flew frequent reconnaissance missions over mainland China (also known as the People's Republic of China) and often passed this valuable intelligence on this Cold War foe on to the U.S. military and CIA.

Several Slick Chicks were lost to enemy fire over China, thus necessitating the need for improved survivability modifications to Taiwan's F-100 fleet. The modifications consisted of altering the F-100A's vertical stabilizer surface to that of the D model, employing the AN/APS-54 tail warning radar, and other changes that enabled the existing Super Sabres to carry and fire Sidewinder air-to-air missiles for defense.

FRANCE

France was the first foreign country to receive the Super Sabre. On 1 May 1958, the French received their first F-100Fs, with a subsequent shipment of the D-version Huns, which arrived on 18 May 1958. The French Air Force (Armée de l'air) soon included eighty-five F-100Ds and fifteen F-100Fs. These aircraft were soon assigned to several escadres (equivalent to the U.S. Air Force fighter group), which at the time were detached to the NATO 4th Allied Tactical Air Force stationed at leasing bases in West Germany.

The French made prudent use of their newly acquired Huns. The French flew their F-100s in earnest until 1966, then transferred the remaining aircraft to

French F-100F s/n 56-4009 prior to being applied a fresh coat of camouflage. *Courtesy David W. Menard*

Escadre 11. That unit supported two active squadrons at the time. Operation of the Hun for these units continued until 1978.

In January 1975, the French initiated a modification program at Châteauroux, raising the F-100 fleet's life expectancy from 4,200 hours to 5,000 hours. All F-100s were eventually retired and replaced by Jaguars. During the replacement phase, all existing F-100s were turned over to the United States. But most of the French Super Sabres never made it home—they were scrapped in the United Kingdom. The F-100 Super Sabre served the French and their interests well, and at that time was the only deep-strike, in-flight refuelable aircraft at their disposal.

This particular example of a French F-100D was carrying both air-to-ground and air-to-air ordnance. *Courtesy Jay Miller Aviation History Collection*

F-100D s/n 55-3535 carrying finned napalm rocket pods and 335-gallon fuel tanks cruises over South Vietnam in mid-1965. *USAF via David W. Menard*

CHAPTER SEVEN

F-100F WILD WEASEL

THE GENESIS OF THE WILD WEASEL concept bore fruit directly from the onset of the U.S. Air Force's involvement in the conflict in Southeast Asia. The communists drew first blood against the air force on 24 July 1965 when a flight of four McDonnell F-4 Phantom IIs flying a MIGCAP (MiG combat air patrol) out of Ubon, Thailand, were fired upon by a Russian-built SA-2 surface-to-air missile (SAM) battery while en route to Hanoi. The trio of missiles found their mark, destroying one Phantom and damaging the remaining three.

It was evident at that time that the North Vietnamese air defense system was growing and improving. Their basic anti-aircraft infrastructure consisted of a widespread and integrated radar network linked to squadrons of MiG-17 and MiG-21 interceptors, further supplemented by optically directed large- and small-caliber antiaircraft artillery (AAA). Subsequent aerial reconnaissance flights over North Vietnam in the proceeding months indicated growing installations of what was thought of as SAM-2 batteries.

The Russian SA-2 anti-aircraft missile air defense system's initial use was to attack large formations of bombers operating at high altitudes. The system lacked the maneuverability to harass tactical aircraft operating at lower altitudes. The missile was powered by a single solid-propellant booster guided by a liquid-fueled sustainer rocket, which took its steering commands from tracking data generated from ground radar systems in the form of computed codes. The missile was not accurate enough to hit the moving aircraft, but rather it was

A 188th TFS New Mexico Air National Guard F-100C on a flight from Clark Air Base, Philippines, to Tuy Hoa Air Base. *Col. Albert Piccarillo*

A 510th TFS F-100D prepares to taxi out to her revetment at Bien Hoa Air Base while carrying four low-drag bombs. *T/Sgt. Norman E. Taylor*

This 3rd TFW F-100D has just released two low-drag bombs on a South Vietnamese target in early 1966. *Courtesy Jay Miller Aviation History Collection*

equipped with a proximity fuse, which detonated within lethal range of the target.

This was the same SA-2 missile system that in part had commanded the attention of the United States during the 1962 Cuban missile crisis. The SA-2s were part of the ring of defenses that protected the Soviet intermediate-range ballistic missiles (IRBMs). These IRBMs were capable of reaching major cities along the Eastern seaboard and were of paramount concern. The first indication of the SA-2's usefulness as a potent antiaircraft system was realized on 1 May 1960 when one such missile shot down pilot Francis Gary Powers' Lockheed U-2 spy plane over the Soviet Union. The missile

Three F-100Ds release their ordnance on the same command over South Vietnam. *Courtesy Jay Miller Aviation History Collection*

certainly had its share of deficiencies. It could not realize its maximum speed of Mach 2.5 until it had achieved an altitude of 25,000 feet and beyond.

By today's standards, the SA-2 was relatively unsophisticated, but, at that time in history, it was state of the art enough to cause grave concerns among U.S. pilots. The mere existence of the few identifiable sites in North Vietnam was enough to warrant the attention of General William C. Westmoreland, commander of U.S. forces in South Vietnam. However, the secretary of defense circumvented Westmoreland's direct actions to eliminate the SAM installations. On 24 July 1965, the U.S. Air Force lost its first aircraft to SA-2 missiles in Vietnam. Only by this admission did the politicians loosen their grip on the military's authority. However, the U.S. government further stipulated tight restrictions, barring U.S. aircraft from violating three special areas. They included a 20-nautical-mile encirclement of Hanoi, an 8-mile circle around Haiphong, and a 10-nautical-mile circle around Phul Yen. Further adding insult to injury, the political war planners in Washington demanded that no SAM site be eliminated without firsthand photo identification by low-flying reconnaissance aircraft.

ARRIVAL OF THE WILD WEASEL

Brigadier General K. C. Dempster, deputy for operational requirements for the U.S. Air Force, became acutely aware of events quickly unfolding in Vietnam and was appointed to lead a task force to secure

Top right: An F-100F of the 429th TFS with two 450-gallon tanks fitted sits in a line with several F-100Ds of the 478th TFS. *Doug Henderson via Jay Miller Aviation History Collection*

solutions to overcome North Vietnam's potent air defense system. Some of the ideas generated were to fly in at low altitudes and conduct bombing runs to knock out suspected SAM sites. This, in fact, proved much too risky due to the aircrafts' proximity at low altitudes to anti-aircraft guns protecting the sites. Other ill-conceived ideas included directing formations of four aircraft to the target at timed intervals consisting of anywhere from one to three minutes. The task force abandoned this idea because of the lack of overall support to aircraft in actual contact with the missile batteries. Often, attacking aircraft had to perform violent maneuvers to evade destruction from the incoming missiles. Attacking aircraft jettisoned weapons to avoid structural failure during the maneuvers.

During the research conducted by the Dempster Task Force, it was discovered that the SA-2 missile possessed some inherent flaws. One such weakness lay in

Above: A three-ship formation of one F-100F and two F-100Ds of the 110th TFS, Missouri Air National Guard, flies over Missouri.

its guidance radar. The radar system generated signals between the launch site and target. It could be jammed with little effort if the right frequency could be found and equipment used. Also, intelligence reports touted the possibility that Russian-built SAM radar sites were in short supply.

The Dempster Task Force, after careful review and painstaking effort, finally concluded that radar homing and warning (RHAW) equipment should be installed in a few F-100F-20 Pathfinder aircraft. This decision was further solidified by the fact that the air force had sufficient numbers of the two-place F-100Fs for immediate modification and use in Southeast Asia. Various radar jamming and homing systems were tried in the F-100, but they proved too bulky and heavy to afford the aircraft and its crew any immediate benefits.

It was not until the introduction of the transistor and the task force's discovery of a company named Applied Technology, Inc. (ATI) that a lightweight system finally materialized. Richard Hartman, program director of ATI, provided working demonstrations of

An F-100D with "snake and nape" breaks left to attack a target in South Vietnam. *Courtesy Jay Miller Aviation History Collection*

A 481st TFS F-100D has just released two 750-pound bombs off her outboard pylons over a target over South Vietnam in 1965. *Courtesy Jay Miller Aviation History Collection*

the firm's IR-133 radar warning receiver, missile-launch detector, and radar-tuned intercept receiver to the Dempster Task Force with stunning results. A letter contract was immediately sent to and signed by ATI. It stipulated ninety days and $100,000 to complete a functional unit for installation in an F-100F (s/n 58-1231) located at North American's Long Beach Special Operations Unit. The device, as it turned out, was delivered on time and on budget. It experienced no apparent installation problems and performed quite well. As a result, an order was given to modify four more F-100Fs (examples 58-1221, -1226, -1227, -1231, and later, -1206, -1212, and -1232). The equipment used in the Super Sabres was originally designed for use in the Lockheed U-2, but prevailing events in Southeast Asia dictated otherwise.

HOW IT WORKS

This new equipment possessed three basic elements. First, a device warned pilots and flight crew that the aircraft was being tracked by Fan Song (NATO codename for the Soviet radar employed by the North Vietnamese SAM crews). Second, it warned of an imminent missile launch. Thirdly, it provided automatic direction finding of the radar signals emitted at the participating SAM sites. This last function would prove lethal against the missile sites by the later incorporation and use of Shrike missiles.

The Wild Weasel equipment embodied the following four components:

1) AN/APR-25 radar homing and warning receiver. Its primary function was to detect S-band signals transmitted by the SA-2 fire-control radar and its AAA radar. In addition, it could also detect C-band signals

The front cockpit forward instrument panel of an F-100D (similar in Wild Weasel aircraft) shows the typical installation of the APR-25 RHAW system. The system's scope location at the upper left is accompanied by the threat display at the right. *Courtesy Jay Miller Aviation History Collection*

from upgraded SA-2 systems and X band from enemy interceptors. This was accomplished by the use of a threat panel utilizing a three-inch CRT to indicate the bearing of the signal.

2) AN/APR-26. This was a tuned crystal receiver to monitor in the L-band frequency to intercept missile-guidance launch signals. Its cockpit display would indicate trouble with a red warning light launch signal.

3) IR-133 was a panoramic receiver, which was far more reactive in the detection of S-band signals and with greater range than that of the APR-25.

4) KA-60 was a panoramic camera utilized to record all relative physical details of the site, ensuing attack, and aftermath. A dual-track tape recorder was also employed to tape all events occurring, later to be used for training purposes.

This lone warrior, F-100D s/n 59-2910 from the 531st TFS, 3rd TFW, is returning to Bien Hoa. It has an APR-25 threat warning antenna under the inlet and a command radio antenna on the dorsal spine. *Courtesy Jay Miller Aviation History Collection*

Another, more detailed view of the APR-25 RHAW system. This display can categorize the radar threat, anti-aircraft artillery, and airborne intercept launch. *Courtesy Jay Miller Aviation History Collection*

TRAINING

What type of men were selected for this type of duty, steeped in danger? These men were volunteers, mainly from Tactical Air Command squadrons. Two flyers were selected from F-100 units stationed at England Air Force Base (AFB), another pair each from Homestead AFB, Luke AFB, Myrtle Beach AFB, and the fighter-weapons wing at Nellis AFB. A few electronic weapons officers (EWOs) were also transferred from Strategic Air Command B-52 bombers.

All primary training and testing were conducted at Eglin AFB and continued until the first crews were ready. The first advanced crew consisted of Captains Edward B. White and Edward E. Sandelius. The pair was deployed from Eglin on 23 November to Korat Royal Thai AFB on Thanksgiving Day 1965.

An appropriate insignia was considered for this newly formed unit. The image of a mongoose and ferret was already in use, so a weasel was chosen due to its ferocity and fearlessness in battle. The prefix "wild" described the nature and general attitude of the crews performing these hazardous missions. So, the name Wild Weasel was fittingly adopted for these F-100 flyers soon to wreak havoc on unsuspecting SAM sites in North Vietnam.

WEASELING

F-100F Wild Weasels were teamed with Republic F-105 Thunderchiefs to form what were called Iron Hand units. Each unit consisted of one F-100 and four F-105 "Thuds." The F-100 crew would locate and mark SAM sites with rockets launched from a pair of LAU-3 canisters for the F-105 crews to sight, lock on, and destroy.

The fact of the matter was only the top pilots from each unit were chosen to take part in the Iron Hand flights. These pilots accepted the most demanding as well as hazardous missions. An attack was initiated with the Wild Weasel's backseater listening for signals. Here is where their training paid off. The skilled flyers could differentiate between the incoming sounds generated by early-warning radars (a groan of sorts) and the raspy shake sound of a missile-guidance radar being turned on. As inexperienced as the EWOs were at their new cat-and-mouse game, they were trained well enough to tell the difference.

A small CRT scope located in the forward cockpit of the hunting Hun could direct the pilot into the general location of the missile site. The back-seat operator employed the IR-133 receiver to establish a permanent fix on the target, usually within one to two degrees. RHAW gear tuned in, the Wild Weasel

A 116th TFS, Ohio Air National Guard, F-100F sits on the Toledo ramp awaiting her next mission. *Courtesy Jay Miller Aviation History Collection*

An F-100F of the 430th TFS displays her red colors. *Doug Henderson via Jay Miller Aviation History Collection*

would deliberately ride the signal toward the site or sites, marking the area with aerial rockets for the F-105 Thud drivers to initiate their bombing runs.

As risky as this operation seemed, both Hun and Thud pilots became rather proficient at the task. During the next five months, Iron Hand flights destroyed many SAM installations while only losing eleven attacking aircraft. Over 180 SAMs were fired at Iron Hand aircraft during some nineteen thousand sorties flown.

The air force soon replaced the rockets and napalm routinely employed by the Weasels with iron bombs. After a fair complement of missions, it was discovered that the added weight of bombs severely inhibited the performance of the Huns, thus escalating the risk of destruction. After much thought and careful consideration, the air force decided to incorporate the AGM-45A Shrike missile, which was developed in 1961 specifically to counter Soviet radar systems. This new anti-radar missile was the first in a family of weapons equipped with passive homing systems whose sole purpose was to ride the enemy's radar signal back to its source, thus completely destroying it. The advent of the Shrike missile system marked the end of the original F-100F Wild Weasel pioneering crews. New equipment was in development soon to spawn the F-105G Wild Weasel III and F-4 Phantom Wild Weasel IV aircraft. Because of the F-100F's supersonic capability and crew of two, it would soon find another use in the escalating war in Southeast Asia.

MISTY FORWARD AIR CONTROL (FAC)

By the time of the Vietnam conflict, air warfare had become very complicated. Ongoing aerial intelligence was a vital part of battle. In Vietnam, the job of aerial intelligence was often performed in slow, piston-engine spotter planes—light aircraft like Cessnas. They were vulnerable, slow, and basically defenseless, and were susceptible to antiaircraft fire. These aircraft performed forward-air-control (FAC) duties—marking targets, directing strikes, correcting weapons deliveries, and, if still flying, reporting the results.

Probably, the last significant duty the F-100Fs performed in Vietnam was that of the forward air controller. The F-100F was superior in most all respects to earlier FAC aircraft employed in Vietnam. The idea of utilizing the remaining F-100Fs in Vietnam in FAC duty materialized as the brainchild of General William W. Momyer. The FAC could ride in the back seat of the Hun and direct traffic. Because of the Super Sabre's superior speed, survivability was vastly improved.

FAC personnel were skilled, organized observers who, with trained eyes and cameras, would fly in over target areas low and fast and report target information to an airborne battlefield command and control center (ABCCC). The ABCCC personnel would direct strike-fighters to the FAC, who would, in turn, mark the targets and direct the attacks.

The call sign given to the newly formed FAC crews flying the F-100Fs came from a song that Major George Day and his wife liked at the time called "Misty" and

Maintenance personnel prepare a 428th TFS F-100F for her next flight. *Doug Henderson via Jay Miller Aviation History Collection*

A 112th TFS, Ohio Air National Guard, F-100F, s/n 56-3990, sits at rest. *Courtesy Jay Miller Aviation History Collection*

was an immediate hit with the unit. In a short period, Misty FAC mission planners standardized the crew procedures, putting equally qualified pilots in the front and back seat. The flyers would alternate between missions.

A typical mission was preplanned on the ground. The pilot in the back possessed all the maps, handled the camera, and did the initial vectoring through communications with the ABCCC (call sign "Hillsboro"). When the strike force arrived, the front-seat pilot would take over, firing markers and directing the strike. A typical mission would consist of two rounds of reconnaissance and two refuelings, often with an extra reconnaissance so as not to overlook anything.

The Misty FAC operation ended shortly after the summer of 1970. The crews involved logged more than 21,000 hours of combat time. The FAC mission still continued, with Wolf FAC of the 8th Tactical Fighter Wing (TFW) out of Ubon, Thailand; Stormy FAC from the 366th TFW, Da Nang; and Tiger FAC of the 388th TFW, Korat, Thailand, operating mostly F-4D Phantoms. In spite of the odds these pilots faced, and aggravated by the U.S. government's constant restrictions levied against them, all the pilots survived.

An F-100F s/n 56-3740 of the 131st Fighter Squadron (FS), Massachusetts Air National Guard, performs a low pass without its external fuel tanks, possibly indicating a test flight after extended maintenance. *Courtesy Jay Miller Aviation History Collection*

The third prototype F-107A, s/n 55120, lifts off from Rogers Dry Lake on a routine test flight. *Courtesy San Diego Aerospace Museum*

CHAPTER EIGHT

F-100B/F-107A: THE OTHER "HUN"

THE STORY OF NORTH AMERICAN'S most promising aeronautical endeavor, the F-100B—or better known as the F-107A—to this day is shrouded in mystery. Highly developed for its time, and far superior to its rival, the Republic F-105 Thunderchief, the revolutionary aircraft was somehow glossed over by the air force in favor of the "Thud." It was rumored that Republic Aviation was in dire need of a defense contract to keep its doors open for business. Nevertheless, this does not diminish the F-107A's capabilities in any way, but it makes one wonder what the aircraft could have truly achieved.

Because of the initial shortcomings of the F-100A, the air force greatly encouraged NAA to design an improved version of the fighter. Touted as the answer to the air force's request, the F-100B project received official authorization on 4 March 1953. NAA's planning and management established Engineering Study Order (ESO) 713 and estimated on 11 March 1953 that the F-100B design would require at least 7,500 engineering hours, which was later revised to 18,800 hours total.

On 22 May 1953, specification number NA 53-389 defined the F-100B design parameters. From its inception, the F-100B would be an evolution of the F-100A Super Sabre. The redesigned aircraft could be placed into production as soon as 1955. The specification requested a faster F-100A day fighter employing a program of aerodynamic drag and weight requirements to enhance performance, especially from its basic airframe and its J57 turbojet engine.

This exploded view is of the F-100B early on in its conceptualization phase of the program. It was later abandoned in favor of NA 212. *Courtesy San Diego Aerospace Museum.*

DESIGN GENESIS

The initial design platform retained the F-100A's wings, further reducing their thickness from 7 percent to 5 percent t/c ratio and employing the area rule concept to its fuselage, further increasing its fineness ratio. The F-100B would be powered by an upgraded version of the J57 fed by a variable-area inlet duct, the Pratt & Whitney J75-P-11 turbojet. Interestingly, the duct for the new fighter would be located on top of the fuselage, aft of the plane's canopy. The J57 would be controlled by a convergent, divergent nozzle, and the entire aircraft was designed to bear the weight of 1,160 gallons of jet fuel. Sturdy landing-gear wheels insured operations from unprepared fields. The F-100B was envisioned as retaining the same weight and size as its predecessor, the F-100A. Preliminary design estimates projected a speed potential of Mach 1.8. At the same time, this presented some problems in aerodynamic kinetic heating.

To further enhance the F-100B's usefulness, NAA also explored the possibility of an all-weather interceptor as stipulated in specification number NA 53-425. The air force officially requested this on 3 June 1953. In addition, this specification requested a modification to the cockpit; the addition of a radome, rocket armament, and heated leading edges; and arrangements for external wing tanks. The fuselage was redesigned, with the distinctive bifurcated inlet located on the top side of the forward section of the fuselage.

On 20 October 1953, the F-100B was re-designated NA 212, which initiated engineering to a budget expenditure totaling $78,000. Within the confines of an additional thirty days, NAA management elected to include its much-discussed fighter-bomber capabilities into its overall design architecture. On 18 November 1953 specification NA 53-1098 stipulated eleven configurations for the aircraft. The versatile F-100B could be adapted to assume the role of air-superiority fighter or fighter-bomber. To accommodate the latter role, engineering added six hard points to the wing and significantly altered the plane's structure, which necessitated the need to change the flight controls and overall cockpit design, while retaining its intended design load factor of 7.33 for the fighter version.

This F-100B drawing was an early construct of study NA 212 and was later revised incorporating the top-mounted bifractured duct. *Courtesy San Diego Aerospace Museum*

The load factor was lowered for the fighter-bomber version, which depended greatly on the external fuel and munitions it would carry.

Other changes the air force requested included incorporating single-point refueling capabilities, upgraded radio equipment, and a canopy further refined to improve pilot vision. The flight-control system was also upgraded by the addition of pitch and yaw dampers.

STRUCTURE

The fuselage of the F-107A was all-metal stressed skin semi-monocoupe construction employing the use of aluminum and titanium. The fuselage was built in two sections: The forward half of the fuselage housed the radome, the cockpit, the wing attachment box structure, and the air inlet duct. The aft portion of the fuselage was constructed mainly from titanium in order to cope with the high temperatures generated from the use of its J75-P-11 turbojet. Both sections were joined by four union-type threaded couplings strategically spaced on the bulkhead located at fuselage station 504.0. Most hydraulic and fuel connections were facilitated by the use of quick-disconnect couplings. The fuselage structure was stressed for positive-13 and negative-4.5 Gs. Operating limits bordered on positive-8.67 and negative-3.0 Gs.

WING

The wing, in accordance with the entire structure, was also fabricated in the semi-monocoupe style of construction. The 45-degree swept wing was orchestrated by employing four basic components: the leading-edge slat assembly; the milled-skin "box," which embraced the wing root and the center section of the wing; the wing center section, which solidified both wing halves;

This drawing reveals the final dimensions and overall aircraft architecture for the F-100B, or now the F-107A. *Courtesy San Diego Aerospace Museum*

and, the trailing edge, which enclosed the flight controls and trailing-edge flaps.

Both 2024 and 7075 aluminum alloys were utilized in the wing fabrication. A fuel cell was integrated in each wing half starting at the wing root to near wing station 197. The torque box responsible for the wings' inherent strength and subsequent resistance to twisting and bending flight loads was fastened together by ninety-four high-strength chrome-moly tension bolts

A quarter rear shot of aircraft example s/n 55-5118. Notice the gaping hole located at the end of the aircraft soon to accept its thirsty powerplant, the Pratt & Whitney J75. *Courtesy San Diego Aerospace Museum*

edge of the stabilizer. The horizontal stabilizer was a two-piece, all-moveable unit connected by a tubular crossbeam sporting a 45-degree leading-edge sweep. It was constructed of aluminum and aluminum honeycomb materials.

HYDRAULIC SYSTEM

The hydraulic system used to operate the F-107A's flight controls and other systems consisted of three separate 3,000-psi constant-pressure types of units. Of these three, two of the units operated the horizontal stabilizer, vertical stabilizer, spoiler, deflector, and flaps. The third, which consisted of the utility system, was completely independent from the other two and provided service to the actuation of the landing gear fairing doors, wheel brakes, nose-wheel steering, speed brakes, gun drive, gun-purging-system doors, and the air-refueling probe.

FLIGHT CONTROLS

on each side of the box. Due to these specific requirements, each bolt possessed a different grip length and special torque. Finally, the wings were attached to the fuselage by the use of four shear pins strategically placed on the front and rear inboard spans.

The 45-degree vertical stabilizer was of all-metal construction and could be turned at once by the use of a single pivot point located inboard from the leading

The flight system was composed of dual, hydraulically controlled systems that were irreversible and equipped for artificial feel. The total control system touted the latest features in control-surface design, including innovations such as an all-movable horizontal and vertical stabilizer for pitch and yaw control, and a spoiler with slot deflectors provided for improved

This is a quarter front shot depicting the progressive phases in construction of prototype s/n 55-5118. Notice the contrasting shades in color of the fabricated metal denoting the various types used in its fabrication. *Courtesy San Diego Aerospace Museum*

lateral control at all flight speeds. To enhance the already advanced control system, an augmented longitudinal control system (ALCS) was added. The ALCS, or Alice for short, was an electronically controlled, hydraulically actuated system that was, in effect, a rudimentary fly-by-wire system. The F-107A employed automatically actuated wing slats working in unison with hydraulically operated trailing-edge flaps, whose performance was enhanced by some of the engine compressor air being redirected over the flaps. For all practical purposes, the F-107A had the most advanced flight-control system in the world at that time.

DUCT

One of the most distinct physical characteristics of the F-107A was in its variable-area inlet duct (VAID) on the top of its fuselage. It was the most advanced inlet system at that time in the entire world. The duct utilized a two-position (3.25-degree and 22-degree) vertical splitter plate supplemented by four hydraulically powered bypass doors positioned on the fuselage.

VAID was automatically operated, and it controlled the volume of air on demand for the engine. This provided the required airflow, regardless of air speed, altitude, or attitude. The system provided 30 percent more air volume to its powerplant at supersonic speeds than any other fixed-area ducts. It was far more advanced than the duct system used in all the F-100 models. The secret of the ramp's successful operation stemmed from its movable vertical ramps located in the forward portion of the duct. The vertical ramps, positioned at the 3.25-degree minimum ramp angle, provided maximum airflow, while repositioning the ramp angle at 22 degrees provided maximum obstruction. Located along the periphery of the duct channel were 526 flush holes that cooled air collected in a storage chamber that surrounded the aft portion of the duct. Located by the storage area were four flap-type air exits called bypass docks. Their purpose was to fend off or bleed air from the duct to further control airflow in the duct. The phenomenon known as duct buzz was virtually eliminated in the aircraft, thus enhancing the safe and reliable operation of the F-107A.

ENGINE

The powerplant used in the prototype F-107A was the YJ75-P-11. The J75 engine was intended to meet the requirements for the next generation of supersonic aircraft. The engine's basic design was derived from the earlier J57, retaining the same compression ratio, split compressor, and other significant design features. Through the advent of advances in component design, it was possible for the improved J75 to obtain a 50 percent increase in thrust over the J57. This was achieved with a marginal 10 percent increase in overall frontal area. It also obtained substantial reduction in total weight as compared to the earlier J57. The J75, through extensive testing, demonstrated its superior performance at high altitudes and supersonic speeds while retaining low fuel consumption at subsonic cruise. The J75 was the logical choice to power the F-107A.

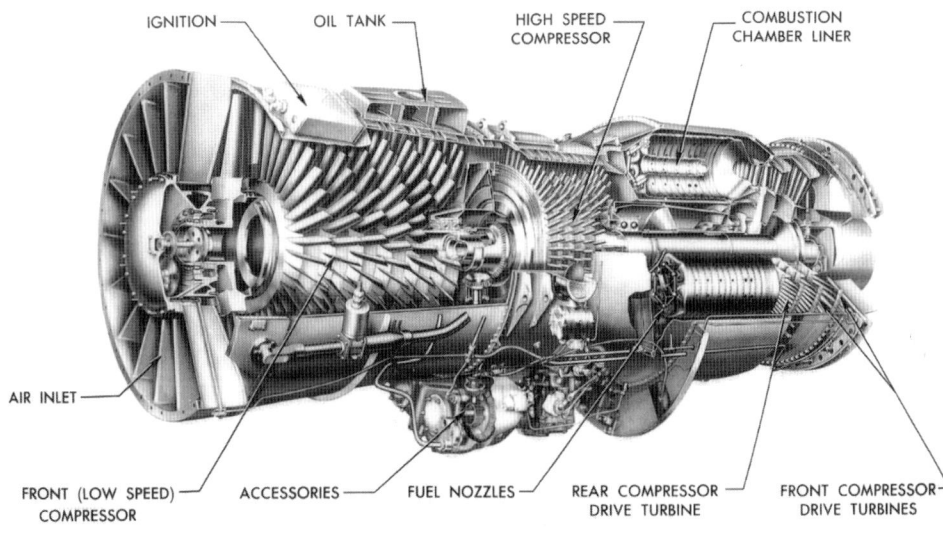

This photo shows the interior components responsible for the proper functioning of the J75. *Pratt & Whitney via Jack Connors*

A cross-sectional drawing of the inner workings of the Pratt & Whitney J75 with afterburner. *Pratt & Whitney via Jack Connors*

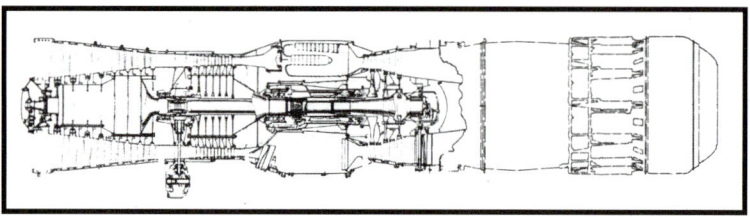

A right quarter shot of the J75 with afterburner fully installed. *Pratt & Whitney via Jack Connors*

MA12 FIRE-CONTROL SYSTEM

In the early developmental stage of the new fighter, the MA12 fire-control system was considered for production F-107As. This system developed by North American's Autonetics Division was state of the art and considered the finest in the world. The system was the first to make full use of air-to-air and air-to-ground radar systems in fighter aircraft. Either visual or radar tracking could be employed, and eventually this entire system was used in the Republic F-105D.

FUEL SYSTEM

Most of the fuel used by the F-107A was located in eight self-sealing bladder-type fuel cells situated in the fuselage at strategic locations. They were supplemented by two integral fuel cells, one in each wing. The eight cells in the fuselage were interconnected to form two tanks. The total internal tankage topped off at 1,260 gallons. Two of the eight fuselage cells were located in the forward section of the fuselage right under the forward end of the intake duct. The other six cells were situated in the rear portion of the airframe under the J75 engine, and were of sump (feed) type.

Provisions were made for a semi-recessed centerline fuel tank to be used incorporating an additional 250 gallons of fuel (1,625 pounds). A pair of 257-gallon tanks could be carried under the wings at station line 100, or two 200-gallon standard U.S. Air Force drop tanks could be carried under the wings at wing station 100 or 155. In-flight refueling was initiated through the extension of a probe-and-drogue system located in the upper left side of the fuselage aft of the cockpit and right above the gun bay. The entire in-flight refueling process could be completed in just four or five minutes. The F-107A also possessed a fuel-purge and venting system consisting of gaseous nitrogen that cleansed the

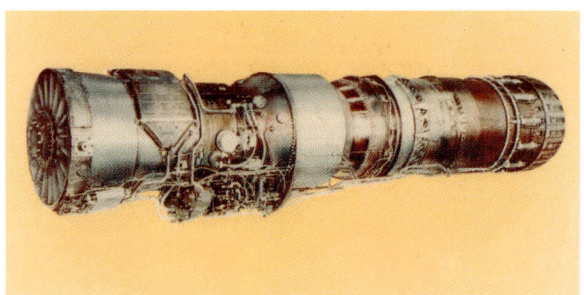

Top left: The Pratt & Whitney J75 (or JT4 civilian designation) with afterburner. Notice how the center section narrows down, incorporating area-rule design. Top right: Cutaway of the J75 without afterburner. *Pratt & Whitney via Jack Connors*

This is F-107A example s/n 55119, fully restored and residing at the Air Force Museum located at Wright–Patterson Air Force Base. *Courtesy San Diego Aerospace Museum*

fuel vapor from all of the fuselage tanks, greatly reducing the risk of any in-flight explosions emanating from unvented fuel.

LANDING GEAR

The F-107A employed a fully retractable tricycle landing gear sporting oleo (gas and oil piston actuated) struts that were electrically sequenced and hydraulically activated. Both the main gear and nose unit fully retracted through forward motion into the fuselage. Total gear extension and retraction transpired in about five to seven seconds for each sequence and was designed with sufficient strength and reliability. Multiple-disc-type hydraulically operated brakes similar to those in use on the F-100 series aircraft provided the stopping power along with two fuselage speed brakes located in the rear portion of the vehicle. The nose-gear steering was fully controlled through the right or left depression of the rudder peddles.

CANOPY

The canopy was composed of one piece and operated on two guide rails in an elevator fashion. Opening of the canopy was initiated by an electromechanical rotary actuator, which raised or lowered a chain attached to the canopy roller support arm. The canopy could be raised a maximum of 26 inches for pilot egress but could only be opened to a mere five inches during engine operation. During an emergency, the canopy was jettisoned by the simultaneous firing cartridge-type charger located around the canopy.

EJECTION SEAT

The unconventional location of the intake duct above the fuselage and right behind the cockpit posed a daunting problem concerning the pilot's egress during an emergency. The ejection seat provided this means and had sufficient power to extract the pilot clear of the jet intake at any speed and altitude. This ejection seat

This picture demonstrates the pilot's ready accessibility to the F-107A (55-5119). The canopy was only fully extended after the engine shut down. *Courtesy San Diego Aerospace Museum*

Example s/n 55-5119 is shown here with canopy in fully extended position. It can be seen why the engine must be fully shut down before the pilot egresses. *Courtesy the San Diego Aerospace Museum*

First prototype s/n 55-5118 lifting off from Rogers Dry Lake around 24 October 1956. *Courtesy Jay Miller Aviation History Collection*

was modeled after the one used in F-100 variants. It was a cartridge-powered catapult mounted vertically behind the seat. During the ejection, the entire seat assembly was guided upward on the seat guide rails. The canopy and seat ejection sequences and systems were totally independent of one another, so, in the event of the canopy failing to jettison properly, the seat could be ejected through the canopy.

OTHER PROGRAM UPDATES

On 15 January 1954, the much-anticipated F-107A program was drastically curtailed at the behest of NAA President Lee Atwood. A memo dated 21 January 1954 stipulated a change from full-production engineering to a Phase 1 comprehensive engineering study to be initiated for the next few months. Full mockups were eventually constructed on 1 May 1954 for the F-100B and on 29 May 1954 for the F-100.

Six days later, the air force expressed intense interest in a fighter-bomber version of the F-100B. In this expression of their intent, the air force suggested changes to alter the overall load factor from 7.33 to 8.67. Late in 1954, the air force issued General Operational Requirement 68 requesting two versions of the F-107A, a tactical fighter-bomber and a day-and-night air-superiority fighter.

Three F-107As were built (AF 55-5118, -5119, and -5120) and were readied for flight testing. The first example flew on 10 September 1956 from Edwards Air Force Base. NAA's new chief test pilot, Bob Baker, performed this flight. He encountered relatively few problems, with the exception of the activation of an oil-pump pressure light, which terminated the first flight early. Overall, the flight-testing program went rather smoothly, with few surprises or outstanding events.

As previously mentioned, the F-107 was in direct competition with Republic Aviation's heavyweight, the F-105 Thunderchief. The Air Force scheduled a fly-off between the two aircraft for the end of 1956. It soon became apparent that the F-105 was having problems and the competitive evaluation would have to be rescheduled for the spring of 1957. The YF-105, as it was known at the time, was experiencing major problems, one of which was its inability to exceed Mach 1. Amazingly, the air force favored this design, even with inherent flaws. In spite of the Thunderchief's shortcomings, the final decision was made in favor of the YF-105 without the much-anticipated fly-off. What was once a promising design, the F-107A faded into obscurity while the Thunderchief would find acclaim over the skies of North Vietnam.

Example s/n 55-5119 is shown here in full flight configuration. It was later proved that the external centerline stores provided minimal drag. *Courtesy San Diego Aerospace Museum*

The first and third F-107 were turned over to the NACA for further research. The first F-107A, s/n 55-5118, was so mechanically unreliable it was relegated to a spare-parts machine. The third example, s/n 55-5120, had a side control stick installed, replacing the centralized control yoke in the cockpit. NASA pilots John McKay, Forrest Peterson, Bob White, and Scott Crossfield all cut their teeth flying that F-107A in preparation for operating the North American X-15 rocket plane. The side stick employed in that aircraft was similar to the control system used in X-15 flight vehicle.

As the story goes, the third example, s/n 55-5120, suffered a catastrophic accident at the hands of Scott

This is a photo of aircraft s/n 55-5120 which was assigned at that time to the VAID program. This was to prove the bifurcated duct's prowess as an air-delivery system for the J75. *Courtesy San Diego Aerospace Museum*

Prototype s/n 55-5119 has been at the Air Force Museum since 1957. Notice its uncharacteristic black radome and its undersized buzz numbers located on its tail. Here she stood for 22 years before undergoing a complete restoration in 1979. *Courtesy Jay Miller Aviation History Collection*

Ship s/n 55-5120 shown here with slats and flaps fully extended in its newly acquired NASA makings quietly resting on the dry lake bed. *Courtesy Jay Miller Aviation History Collection*

Crossfield and was not repaired. The air force junked the unique plane. The first aircraft, s/n 55-5118, found its permanent home in the Pima Air Museum in Tucson, Arizona, and the second example, s/n 55-5119, was sent to the Air Force Museum, located at Wright-Patterson Air Force Base, Ohio.

RF-100A "SLICK CHICK"

At the request of the air force, NAA modified six F-100As to a tactical reconnaissance platform by the removal of the four M39E cannon and ammunition boxes. Additional fabrication was required in order to accommodate the five side- and forward-scanning reconnaissance cameras. This new creation was dubbed "Slick Chick" and was supplemented with four additional wing tanks to extend the plane's range while in full afterburner. There were some flight-control linkage problems that were soon rectified. The Slick Chick served well in its reconnaissance role for NATO countries and Taiwan.

Above front view of example s/n 55-5119 with leading-edge slats fully extended. Also note its area-ruled fuselage and its wing also employed on the F-100D and F Super Sabre as well. *Courtesy San Diego Aerospace Museum*

Front view of RF-100A displays her cheek positions housing the cameras. Also note the auxiliary wing fuel tanks for added range. *North American Aviation via David W. Menard*

Side shot of RF-100A s/n 53-1551 strutting her cheek cameras and the considerable fuselage modifications to enclose this equipment. *North American Aviation via David W. Menard*

ZEL

ZEL stands for zero-length launch system, which was being developed in 1958 by North American Aviation. The concept had its roots back in 1956 when someone at NAA had the bright idea of strapping a powerful, solid-fuel rocket motor large enough to accelerate an F-100 from a dead stop to 275 knots employing 130,000 pounds of thrust for four seconds. The launch of the Hun would originate from mobile platforms located in hardened shelters slated for use in NATO-aligned countries in Western Europe.

The reasoning being ZEL stemmed from the fact that all the NATO air bases were at that time prime targets during the event of a Soviet nuclear first strike. ZEL could offer NATO retaliation, capability, and some degree of stealth. The Soviets could not target all the ZEL dispersal sites throughout Europe. ZEL also offered the U.S. Air Force's F-100 and other Century Series aircraft independence from the use of a 10,000-foot concrete runway. The ZEL test program met with moderate success but, for reasons still unclear, was never fully embraced or accepted. Therefore, the ZEL program was relegated to the back pages of history.

Forward view of a ZEL-launched F-100D. Notice the asymmetrical wing-tank position. The original photo sported a tactical nuclear munition positioned on the left wing which fell prey to an artist's air brush for security reasons. *Courtesy Jay Miller Aviation History Collection.*

APPENDIX A

SPECIFICATIONS

All F-100 models

	YF-100	F-100A	F-100C	F-100D	F-100F
Wingspan	36' 7"	38' 9"	38' 9"	38' 9"	38' 9"
Length	46' 3"	47' 1"	47' 1"	47' 1"	50' 4"
Fuselage (excluding pitot boom)					
Height	14' 5"	15' 4"*	15' 4"	16' 2"	16' 2"
Wing area (sq ft)	376	385	385	400	400
Weight					
empty (lb)	18,135	18,135	19,270	20,638	21,712
(kg)	8,226	8,226	8,740	9,361	9,848
combat (lb)	24,789	24,996	28,700	30,061	31,413
(kg)	11,244	11,338	13,018	13,635	14,248
gross (lb)	28,561	28,899	36,549	38,048	39,122
(kg)	12,955	13,108	16,578	17,258	17,745

*(F-100A with 'short' vertical stabilizer was 13' 4")

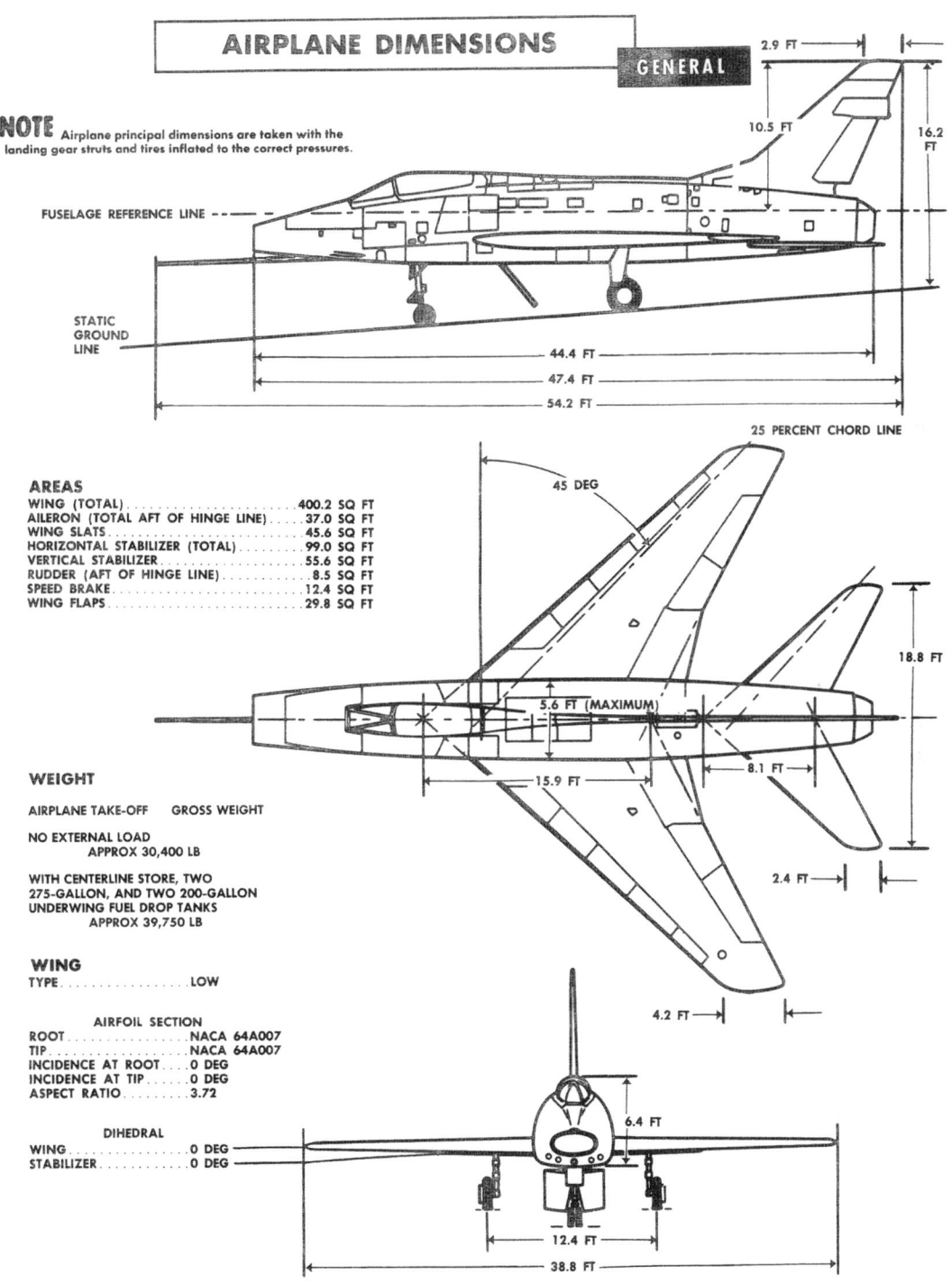

Dimensions: F-100D

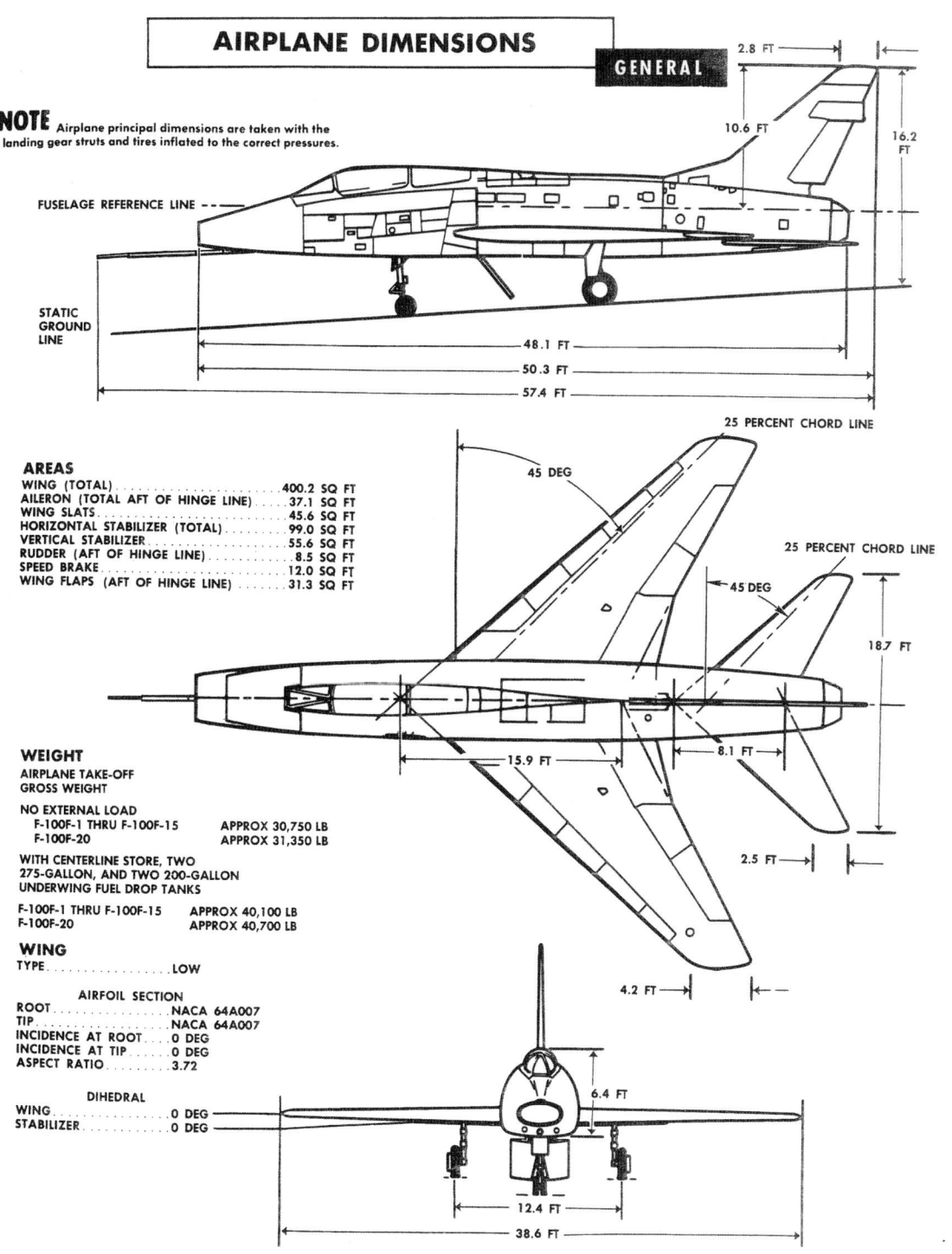

Dimensions: F-100F

APPENDIX B

PRODUCTION LIST

Note: The following lists of block numbers are shown as ordered. In 1963 and 1964, all F-100 block numbers were increased by one during Project Hi-Wire. For example, F-100A-5-NA became F-100A-6-NA, F-100C-25-NA became F-100C-26-NA, etc.

F-100A:
F-100A-1-NA	52-5756 through 52-5765
F-100A-5-NA	52-5766 through 52-5778
F-100A-10-NA	53-1529 through 53-1568
F-100A-15-NA	53-1569 through 53-1608
F-100A-20-NA	53-1609 through 53-1708

F-100C:
F-100C-1-NA	53-1709 through 53-1778
F-100C-1-NA	54-1740 through 54-1769
F-100C-5-NA	54-1770 through 54-1814
F-100C-15-NA	54-1815 through 54-1859
F-100C-20-NA	54-1860 through 54-1970
F-100C-25-NA	54-1971 through 54-2120
F-100C-10-NH	55-2709 through 55-2733

F-100D:
F-100D-1-NA	54-2121 through 54-2132
F-100D-5-NA	54-2133 through 54-2151
F-100D-10-NA	54-2152 through 54-2221
F-100D-15-NA	54-2222 through 54-2303
F-100D-20-NA	54-3502 through 54-3601
F-100D-25-NA	55-3602 through 55-3701
F-100D-30-NA	55-3702 through 55-3814
F-100D-35-NH	55-2734 through 55-2743
F-100D-40-NH	55-2744 through 55-2783
F-100D-45-NH	55-2784 through 55-2863
F-100D-50-NH	55-2864 through 55-2908
F-100D-55-NH	55-2909 through 55-2954
F-100D-60-NA	56-2903 through 56-2962
F-100D-65-NA	56-2963 through 56-3022
F-100D-70-NA	56-3023 through 56-3142
F-100D-75-NA	56-3143 through 56-3198
F-100D-80-NH	56-3351 through 56-3378
F-100D-85-NH	56-3379 through 56-3463
F-100D-90-NA	56-3199 through 56-3346

F-100F:
F-100F-1-NA	56-3725 through 56-3739
F-100F-5-NA	56-3740 through 56-3769
F-100F-10-NA	56-3770 through 56-3919
F-100F-15-NA	56-3920 through 56-4019
F-100F-15-NA	58-6975 through 58-6983
F-100F-15-NA	59-2558 through 59-2563
F-100F-20-NA	58-1205 through 58-1233

Subtotals:
- YF-100 2
- F-100A 203
- F-100C 476
- F-100D 1,274
- F-100F 339

Total all models: 2,294

APPENDIX C

MODELER'S SECTION

This section is included to aid the hobbyist in producing a model of the F-100 through relevant drawings and cross-sections.

J57-P-7 Turbojet

ENGINE GENERAL INFORMATION

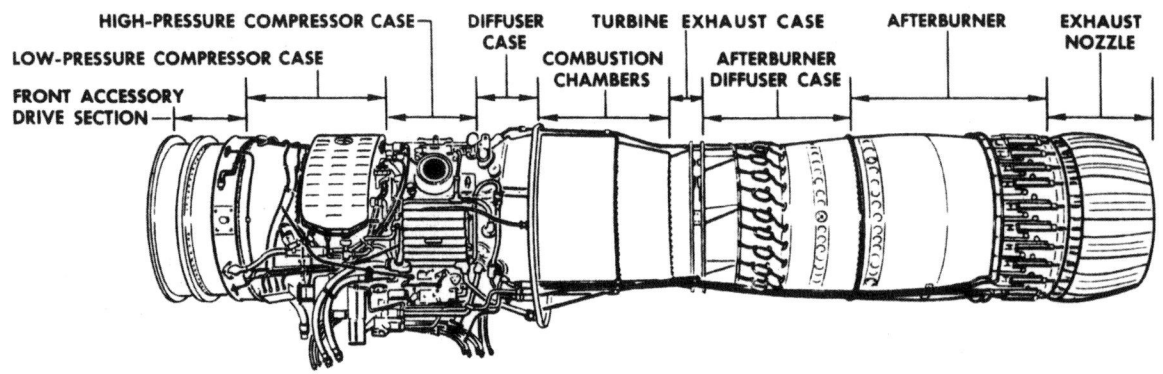

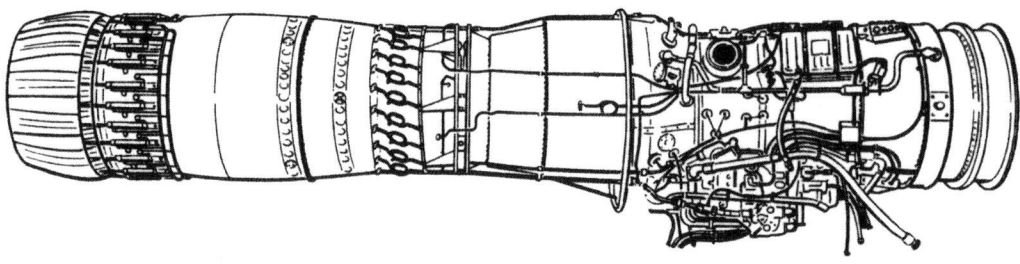

F-100F Fuselage Stations

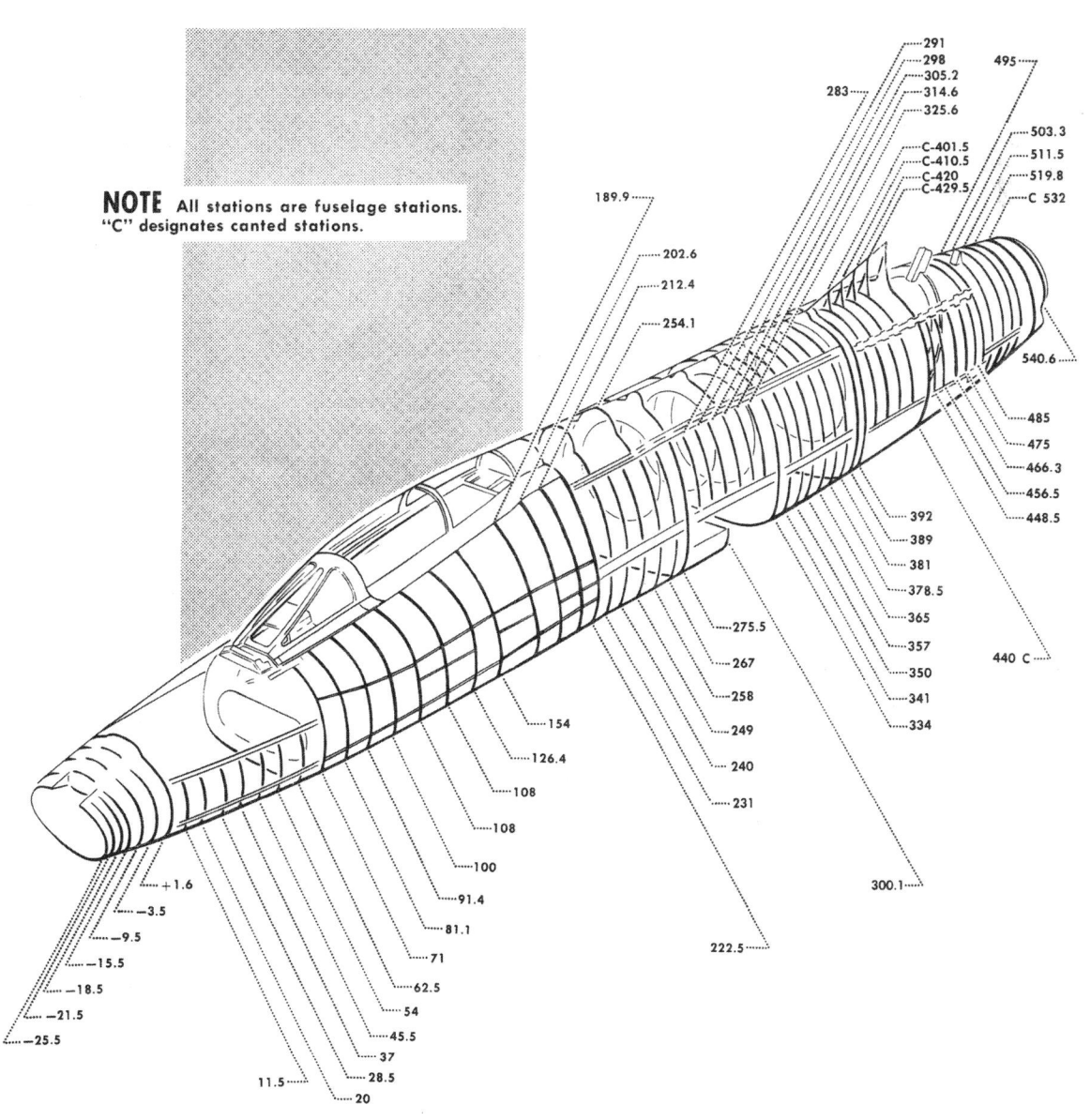

NOTE All stations are fuselage stations. "C" designates canted stations.

F-100D Fuselage Stations

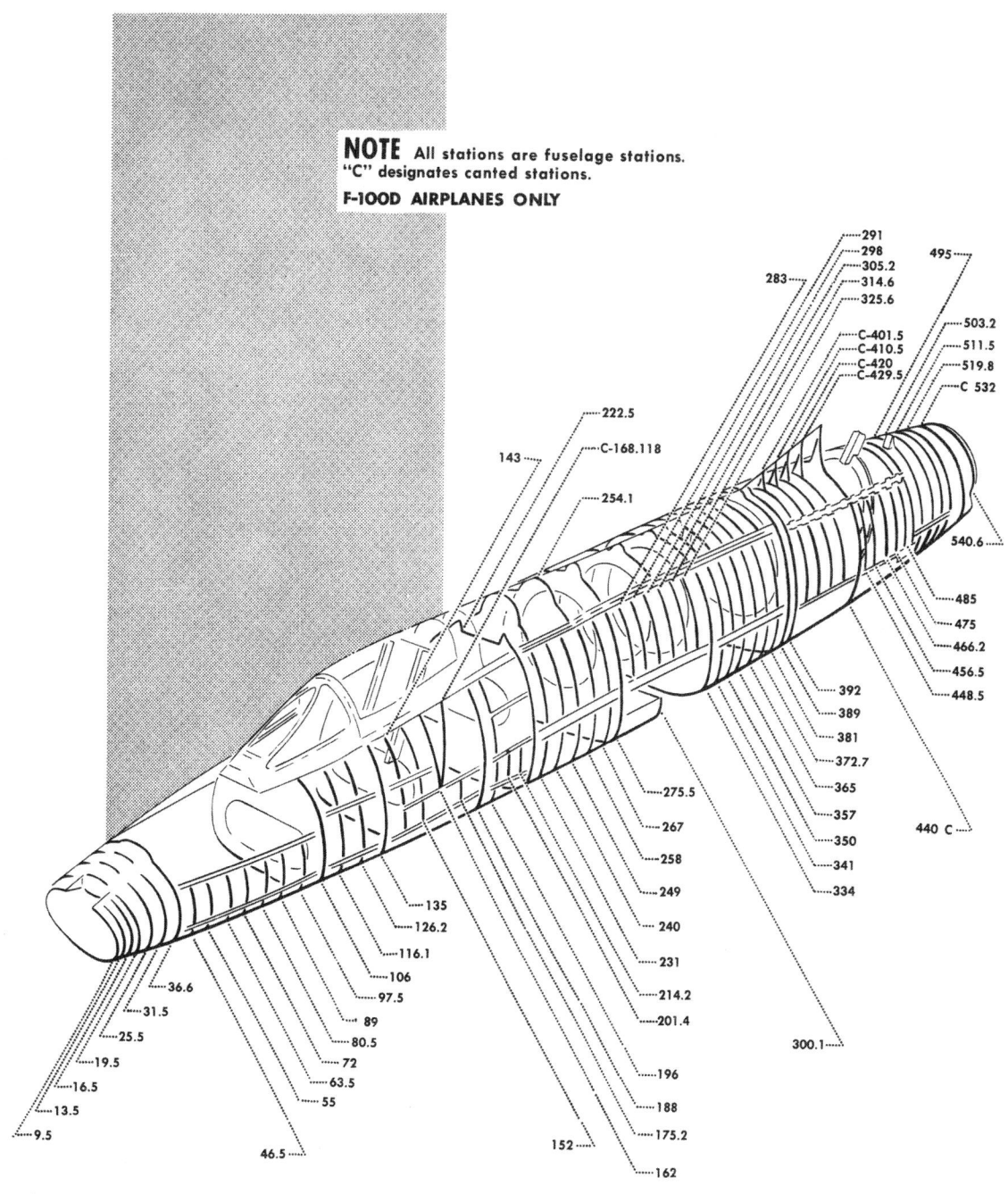

Empennage Stations, F-100D

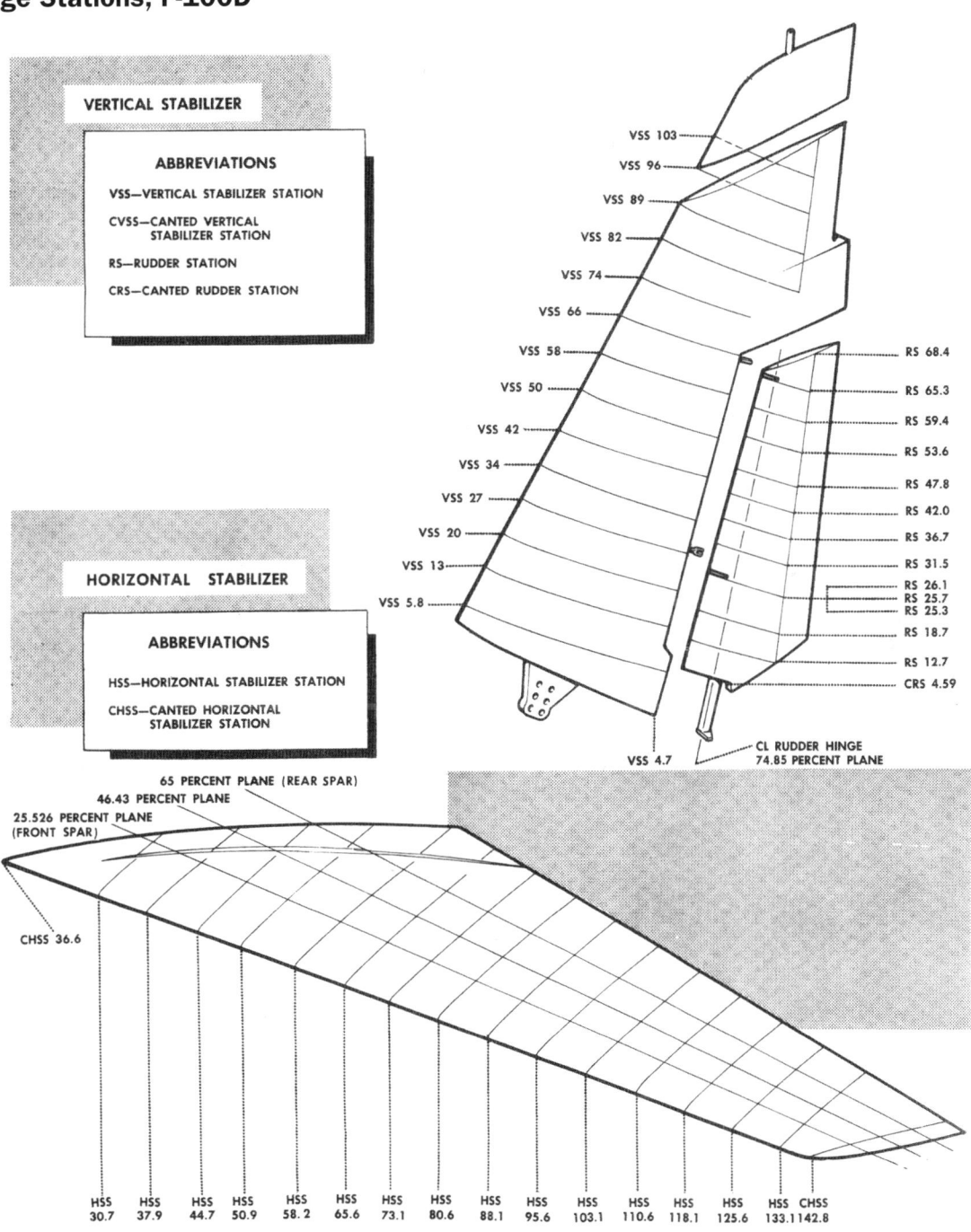

Wing Leading-Edge Stations, F-100D

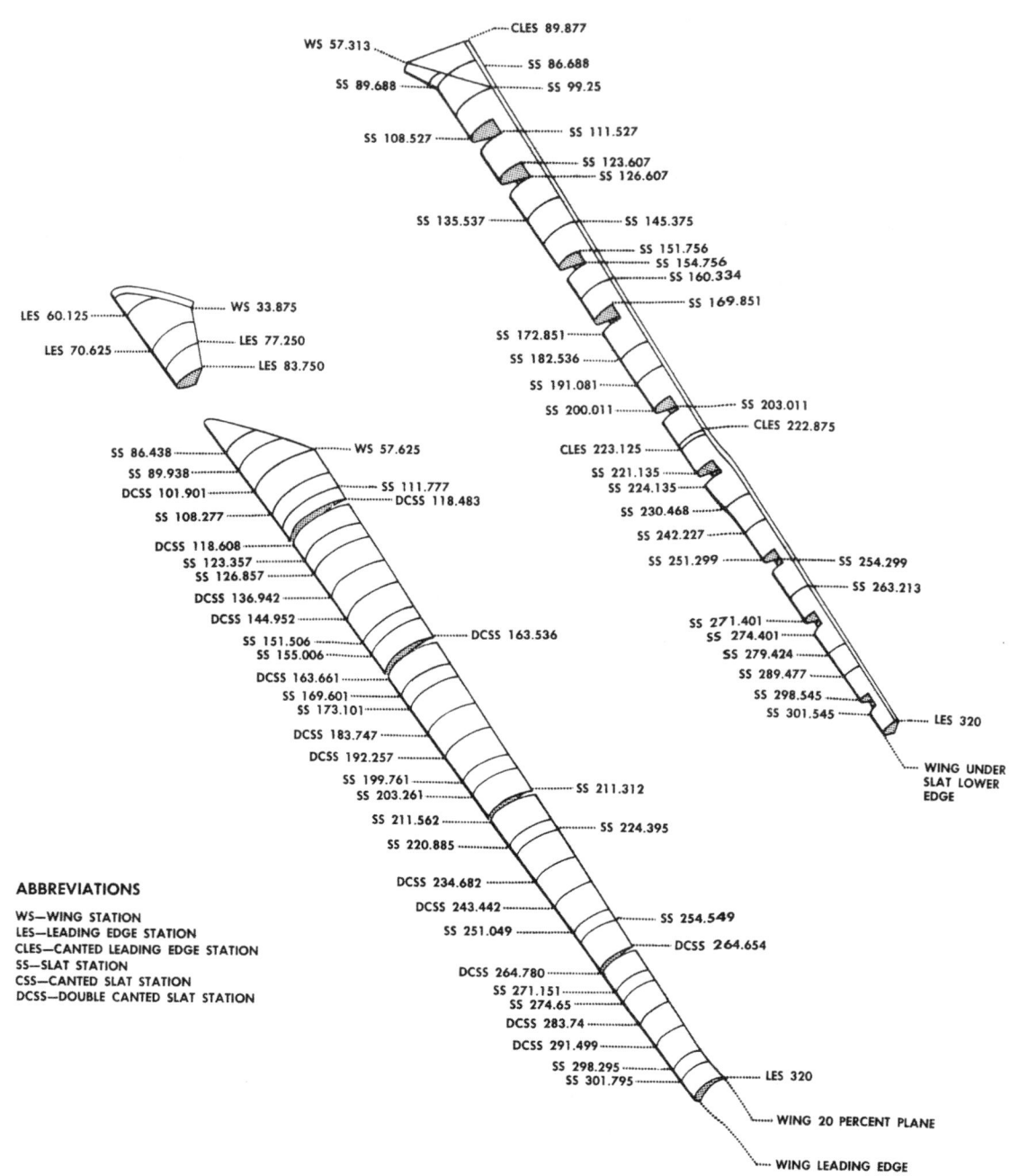

F-100D Reference Planes

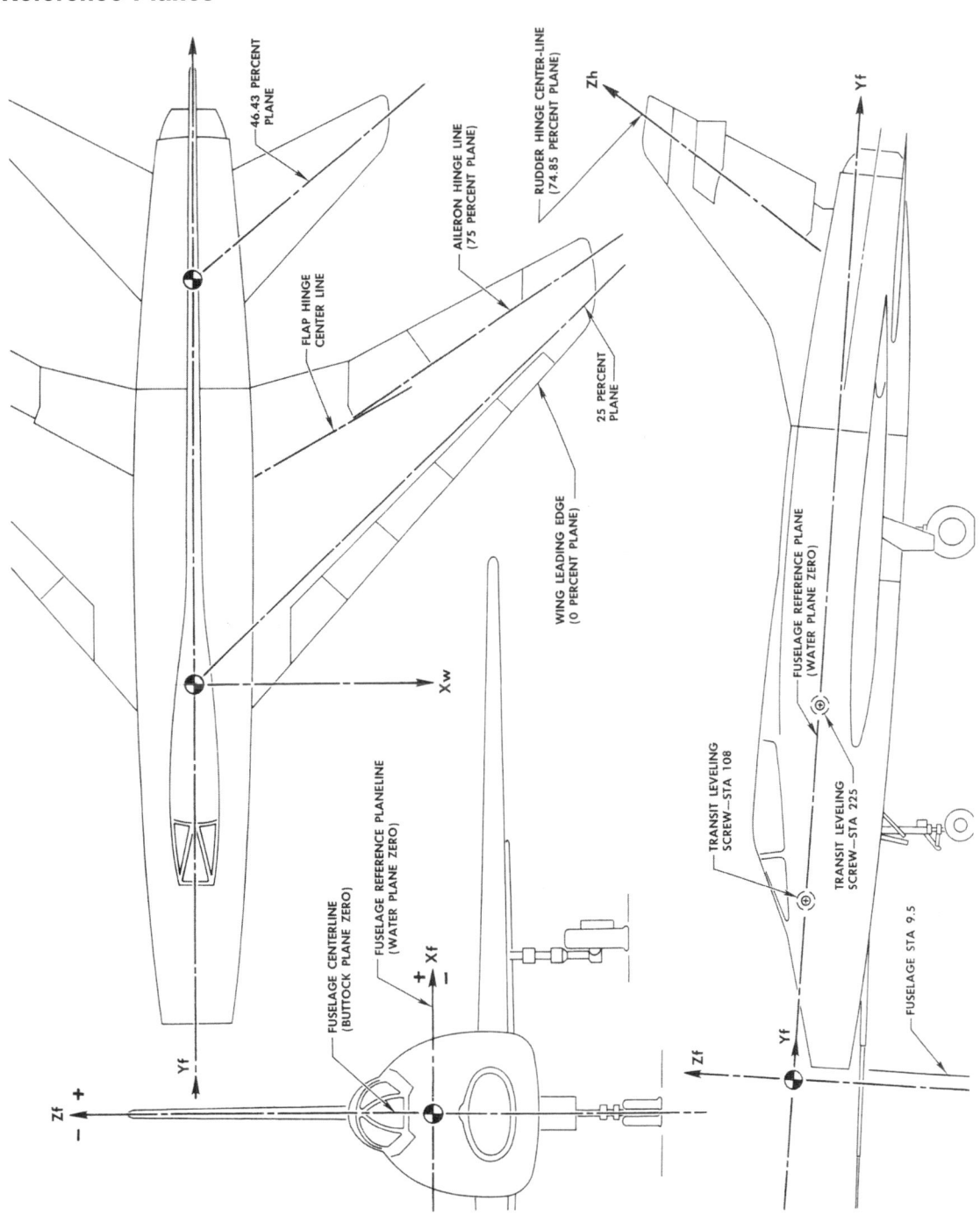

Wing Stations, F-100D

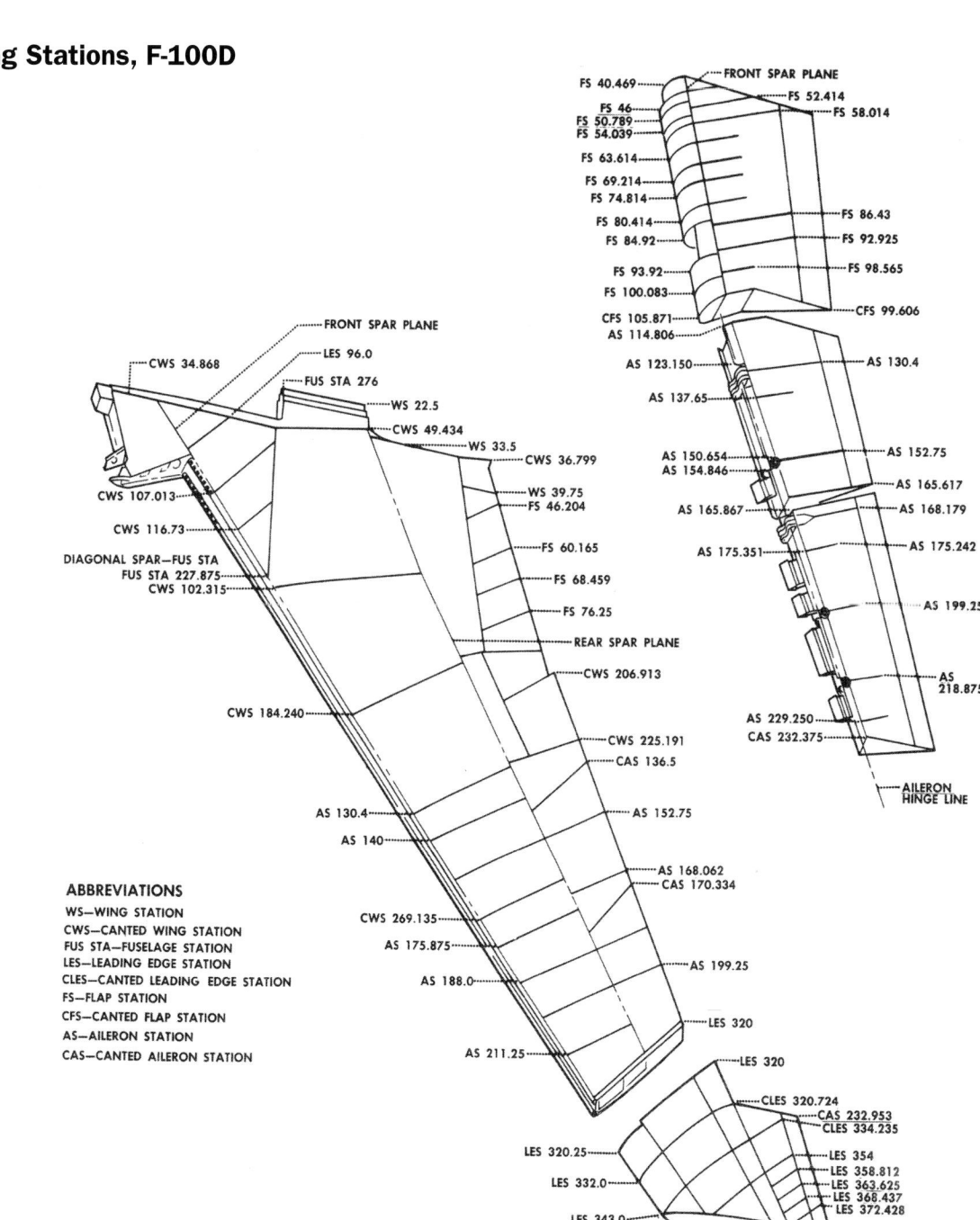

Starboard-Side View with Fuselage Cross-Sections F-100D

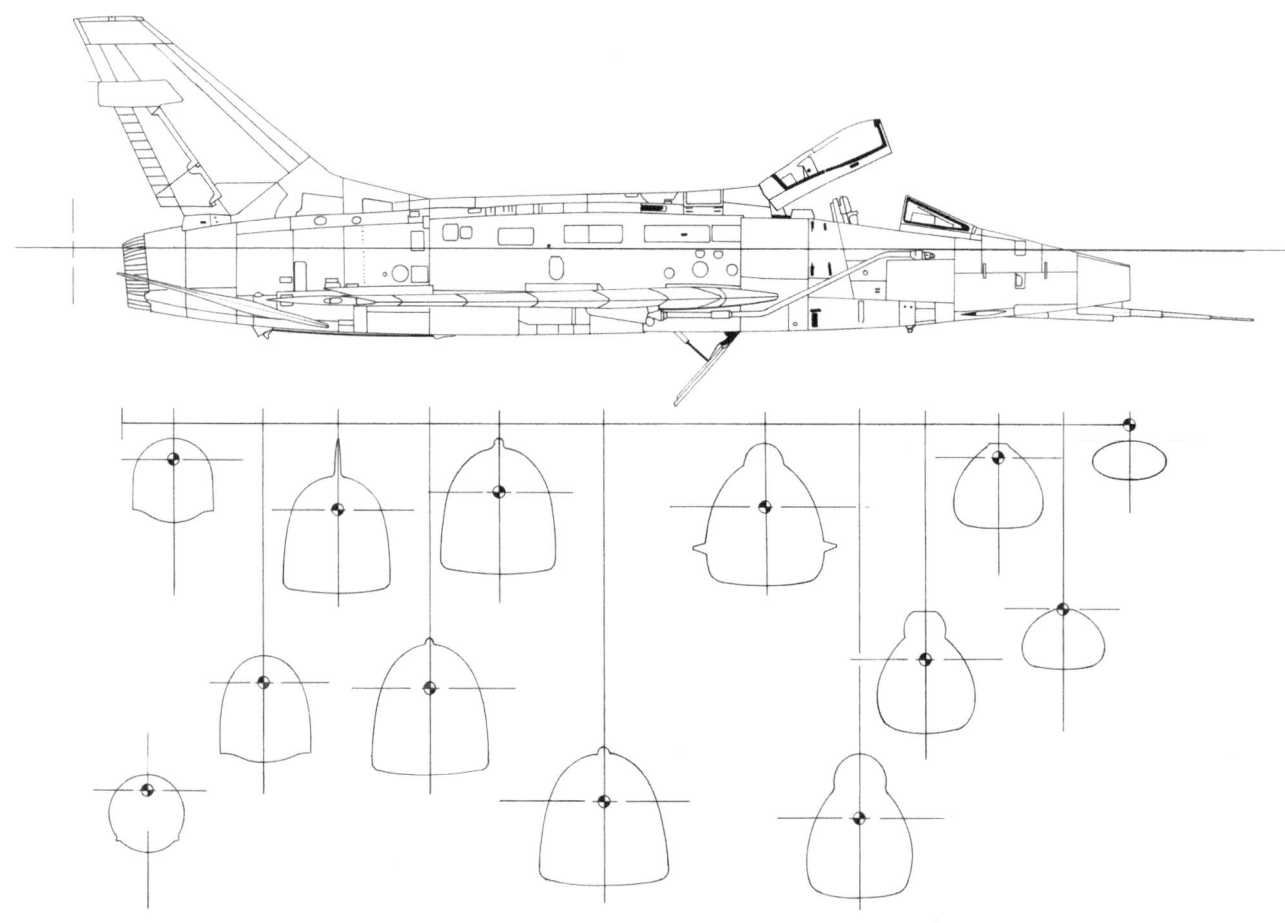

Top View F-100D

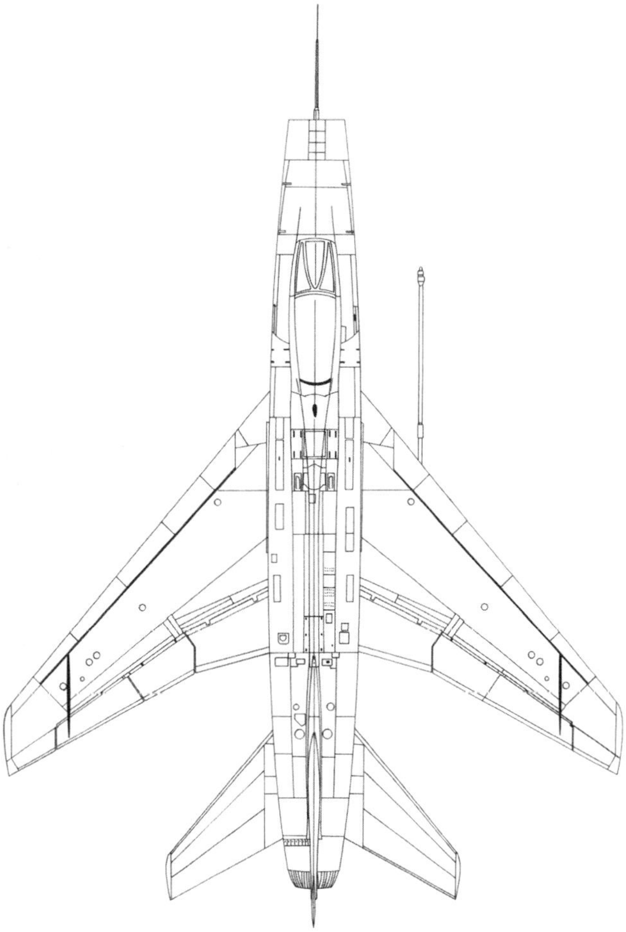

Bottom View F-100D

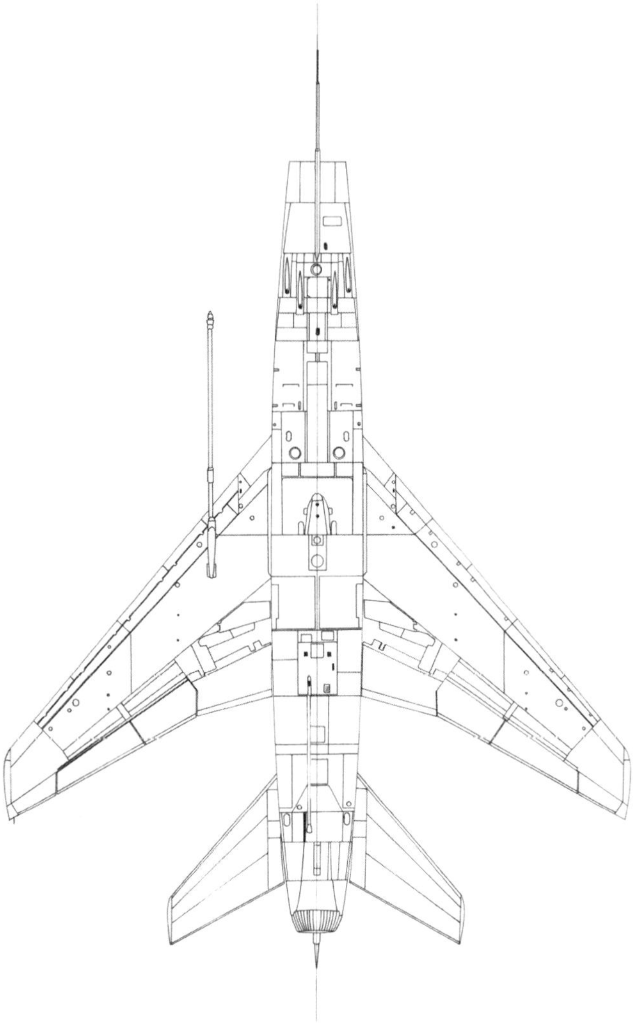

Port-Side View F-100D

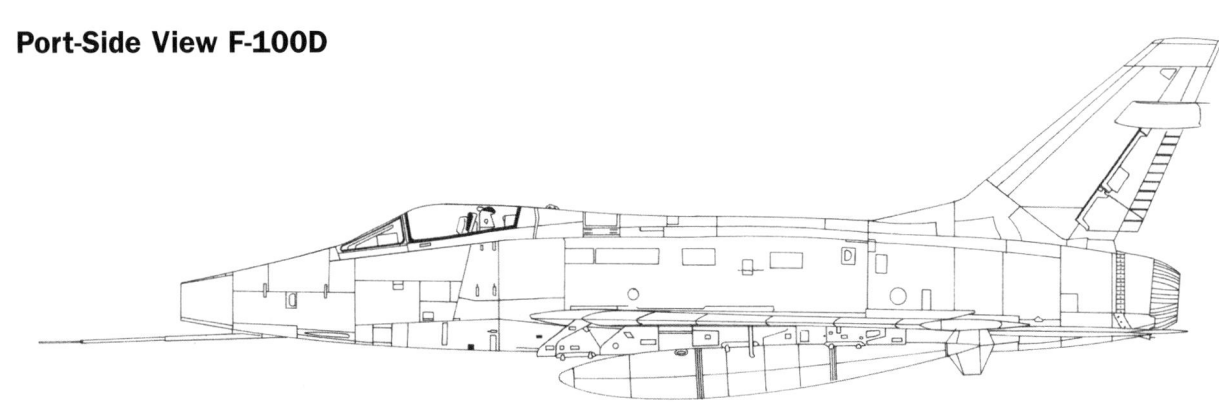

APPENDIX D

SIGNIFICANT DATES

F-100 Program Chronology:

1949 Feb 03: NAA began studies of ways to increase level-flight speed of F-86 design to Mach 1.

Sep 14: Studies showed that a modified F-86D, with a 45-degree sweptback wing and an advanced GE J47 engine, would have a level-flight speed of Mach 1.03. Informal name: Sabre 45.

1950 Aug 25: NAA proposed Advanced F-86D to USAF to meet anticipated need for an interim interceptor (F-102 was in trouble). USAF rejected proposal, but showed interest in advanced day fighter.

Sep: USAF Advanced Development Objective established.

1951 Jan 15: NAA submitted unsolicited proposal of Advanced F-86E to USAF for consideration as advanced day fighter. USAF indicated need for such an airplane as an air superiority fighter.

Jan 19: NAA began self-funded design effort on prototype Sabre 45 air-superiority fighter.

May 14: NAA submitted proposal to USAF to build two prototype Sabre 45 air-superiority fighters. Aim: Achieve early combat availability of production aircraft.

Aug 27: USAF issued general operational requirement for an air-superiority fighter weapons system, with preferred operational date in 1955 but not later than 1957.

Oct: Air Force Council (AFC) urged development of revised version of Sabre 45, although key development personnel believed it could not meet simplicity and cost requirements of a day fighter. AFC also agreed with Aircraft and Weapons Board recommendations to buy in quantity prior to flight-testing (Cook-Craigie Plan), although this ran the risk of a major modification program down the line.

Nov 01: USAF issued letter contract AF 33 (600)-6545, authorizing construction of two Sabre 45 prototypes, engineering design and fabrication of production tooling, and procurement of long-lead-time materials and equipment to build approximately 94 Sabre 45 aircraft.

Nov 09: Mock-up inspection of Sabre 45; air force board identified armament deficiencies, requested modification to increase kill potential, received 100-plus configuration change requests.

A 110th TFS, Missouri Air National Guard F-100D flies over St. Louis. *Courtesy Jay Miller Aviation History Collection*

1951 Dec 07: USAF re-designated Sabre 45 as F-100A.

1952 Jan 25: USAF issued telegraphic amendment to letter contract of 1 November 1951, authorizing unrestricted production of 23 F-100A aircraft, plus one static-test article, plus spare parts, etc. Fiscal Year 1952 funds were used.

Mar 21: Mock-up inspection of F-100A; most changes requested in late 1951 had been made.

Jun 23: Inspection of revised mockup completed by USAF. Extensive design changes to the F-100A had been made in the mockup.

Aug 26: USAF issued Amendment Number 7 to letter contract of 1 November 1951, increasing procurement to 273 F-100A aircraft and one static-test article.

Aug 29: Basic release of 4,118 YF-100A engineering drawings to manufacturing division on schedule. Manpower peak: 878 engineers; total engineering hours expended to date: 984,369.

Dec 29: USAF issued fixed-price contract AF-6545, covering letter contract and amendments issued earlier.

1953 Jan 30: Basic release of 5,701 F-100A drawings to manufacturing division on schedule. Total engineering hours expended to date: 245,551.

1953 Apr 24: First YF-100A completed on schedule by factory.

May 25: First flight, first prototype YF-100A; pilot, George Welch. Time: 55 minutes. Second flight time 20 minutes. NAA claims Mach 1 exceeded on both flights. YF-100A is the world's first operational supersonic airplane.

Sep 17: U.S. Air Force completed YF-100A Phase II flight tests; 39 flights, total duration 19 hours 42 minutes. Offical USAF comment: "... YF-100A-series airplane outperforms any other production fighter in the USAF at this time." Flight tests confirmed three major deficiencies: poor visibility laterally, poor longitudinal stability, and high landing speeds.

Sep 25: First F-100A completed by factory three weeks ahead of schedule. Vertical tail change: YF-100A had t/c ratio of 7 percent; production aircraft had thinner tail, t/c ratio of 3.5 percent.

Oct 14: First flight, second prototype YF-100.

Oct 26: First F-100A acceptance by USAF.

Oct 29: First flight of first production F-100A. Pilot: George Welch; duration: 30 minutes; speed less than Mach 1 in level flight.

A 110th TFS, Missouri Air National Guard F-100D cruises high over Missouri. *Courtesy Jay Miller Aviation History Collection*

1953 Oct 29: First prototype YF-100A set a world speed record of 755.149 mph, last such record established at low altitude. Pilot: LTC F. K. Everest, chief of flight test operations laboratory at ARDC/AFFTC/Edwards AFB. Course: 15 km above Salton Sea. Reached peak speed of 767.337 mph on one run.

Oct–Dec: General strike by NAA labor force.

Dec 08: First F-100A demonstrated high-speed guarantee: Mach 1.34 at 35,000 ft.

Dec 30: Last 70 F-100A aircraft procured under AF-6545 to receive provisions for fighter-bomber missions, and to be redesignated F-100C. Contract now calls for 203 F-100As and 70 F-100Cs. Reason: TAC's urgent need, slippages in F-84F program, requirements of countries in Mutual Development Assistance Program.

Dec: Modifications included addition of black boxes to improve both stability and control in yaw and pitch; additional transparency area added laterally; integral fuel wing tanks (NAA suggestion) for future production aircraft to get range equivalent to that supplied by a pair of 275-gallon external tanks; addition of both nuclear and conventional bomb capability (TAC mid-1953 proposal).

1954 Feb 03: F-100A with "thin tail" (empennage t/c ratio changed to 0.035 on horizontal tail also) flew at Mach 1.35 in level flight at 35,000 ft.

Feb 24: USAF issued letter contract AF 33 (600)-26962, authorizing production of 230 additional F-100C aircraft for total of 300 (other 70 from conversion of last 70 production F-100A aircraft).

Mar 02: USAF Development Engineering Inspection (DEI) Board completed inspection of F-100C aircraft.

Mar 07: F-100C manufacturing began at NAA Los Angeles plant.

Mar 12: F-100A (no. 4) delivered to engineering for modification to dry-wing F-100C prototype.

Mar 26: Basic release of 6,934 old and new engineering drawings of F-100C made to manufacturing. Total engineering hours: 287,837.

Mar: First flight, prototype F-100C.

Apr 14: USAF completed initial Phase II flight test evaluation at AFFTC/Edwards AFB.

May 10: NAA began studies of two-place supersonic trainer.

High above the clouds, this F-100D from the 110th TFS, Missouri Air National Guard, cruises effortlessly. *Courtesy Jay Miller Aviation History Collection*

1954 May 27: USAF issued definitive contract AF 33 (600)-26962 authorizing production of total of 564 F-100C aircraft, an increase of 334 units above the 230 originally authorized under letter contract.

May: TAC request for more-capable fighter-bomber led to USAF studies of third model: F-100D.

Jun 11: USAF issued letter contract AF 33 (600)-27787 authorizing F-100B fighter-bomber design, mockup, and procurement of long-lead-time raw materials for 33 F-100B (later to be redesignated F-107A) aircraft.

Jun 25: F-100A engineering manpower peak of 757 people, including flight test activity, was reached.

Jul: Mockup of F-100BI interceptor completed; design was potential backup for Convair F-102 interceptor, but was not developed because of major deficiencies found during testing of A models.

Aug 15: F-100A manufacturing achieved peak rate with total of 3,740 employees in direct production.

Sep 09: Six F-100A aircraft modified with installations of photo-reconnaissance equipment for special purposes.

1954 Sep 18: First acceptance of unmodified (low-tail) F-100A by TAC.

Sep 27: USAF issued contract change notice to AF-26962, authorizing production of last 224 ships on the 564-ship F-100C contract to be completed as F-100D models. Changes included addition of flaps and certain fighter-bomber aids requested by TAC.

An open house at Turner Air Force Base, Georgia, featured this ornately colored F-100D from the 309th Fighter Bomber Squadron circa 1958. *Courtesy Jay Miller Aviation History Collection*

Sep: USAF decided to accelerate production by opening second source at Columbus, Ohio, and to procure a third model series. Reason: improved Russian fighters.

Oct 01: First F-100A (unmodified, ship no. 47) entered operational service with TAC 479th Fighter Day Wing (FDW), George AFB. Considered an interim aircraft to be replaced by modified F-100A, and subsequently used to introduce TAC pilots to experiences of supersonic flight.

Oct 11: USAF issued letter contract AF 33 (600)-28736 authorizing production of additional 25 F-100C and 221 F-100D aircraft at NAA Columbus, now officially a second production source.

Oct 12: F-100A ship no. 9 destroyed during high-Mach structural demonstration flight. Senior engineering test pilot George Welch killed.

Oct 19: First production F-100C (wet wing) completed.

1954 Oct 29: First F-100C conditionally accepted by USAF.

Nov 10: First F-100A fleet grounding, following six major accidents caused by yaw characteristics, structural failure induced by aerodynamic forces, and malfunction of flight-control system hydraulic pump. Production aircraft coming off line stored to wait modifications.

Nov 15: A number of F-100A aircraft on NAA flight test status were released from grounding order to continue stability-and-control test program.

Dec 06: USAF issued change to F-100A production contract AF-6545, limiting production to 25 completed aircraft per month.

Dec 08: Development Engineering Inspection (DEI) Board completed F-100D inspection.

Dec 17: Collier Trophy awarded to NAA Chairman J. H. Kindelberger for the development of the F-100, the world's first operational supersonic fighter.

An ex-50th TFW F-100D now assigned to the 493rd TFS, 48th TFW, undergoes close scrutiny at an open house at RAF Lakenheath, England. *Courtesy Jay Miller Aviation History Collection*

1955 Jan 17: First flight of first production F-100C (wet wing, P-7 engine).

Jan 26: CDI and CTCI Boards completed inspection of F-100C.

Feb 11: USAF issued change notice to F-100A production contract AF-6545, removing production-rate restriction.

Feb 21: USAF issued contract change notice authorizing modification of all F-100A airplanes. Extensive program scheduled to incorporate approved modifications and to return each F-100A to flight status. Action lifted restrictions of November 54.

Feb 26: NAA Inspection Test Pilot George Smith ejected from F-100A above the Pacific at about 8,000 ft. and Mach 1.05. Suffered massive injuries, but recovered to fly again. Subject of intensive investigation of emergency escape.

Feb 28: F-100D manufacturing began at Los Angeles plant.

Mar 25: Basic release of 7,436 F-100D old and new engineering drawings to manufacturing. Total of 274,100 engineering man-hours expended.

Apr 06: USAF issued letter contract AF 33 (600)-29150 authorizing production of 496 F-100D aircraft.

Apr: Deliveries of aircraft to TAC resumed; production of A-model ended; first F-100C accepted by USAF.

Jul 14: F-100C entered operational service with 450th FDW, later 322nd fighter-day group (FDG), Foster AFB, Texas.

Jul: Last 23 F-100A models accepted by USAF.

1955 Aug 20: F-100C established world speed record of 822.135 mph over 15–25 km course on Mojave Desert, Palmdale, California. Pilot: Col. Horace A. Hanes.

Aug 30: USAF issued letter contract AF 33 (600)-31311 authorizing production of 364 additional F-100D aircraft at NAA Los Angeles plant.

Sep 04: F-100C won Bendix Trophy, 2,325 mi. at average of 610.726 mph.

Sep 02: NAA proposed to modify F-100C to two-seat fighter trainer version at no cost to USAF.

Sep 28: USAF issued contract change notice (CCN 6N-2264) authorizing modification of one government-furnished equipment (GFE) F-100C s/n 54-1966 into a two-place TF-100 supersonic trainer.

Sep: F-100A initial operational capability achieved by 479th FDW. F-100C production aircraft with J57-P-21 engines made first flight.

Nov 14: First F-100D completed by factory and accepted by USAF.

An F-100D of the 110th TFS, Missouri Air National Guard. *Courtesy Jay Miller Aviation History Collection*

Dec 08: USAF issued letter contract AF 33 (600)-31863 authorizing production of 295 F-100F airplanes. F-100D production was reduced simultaneously.

Dec 09: Basic release of 546 TF-100C old and new engineering drawings made to manufacturing. Total engineering hours expended: 48,246.

late 1955: F-100A evaluated in Project Hot Rod by Air Proving Ground Command, rated superior to other fighters in USAF inventory, but of limited tactical capability because of functional deficiencies.

1956 Jan 24: First flight, first production F-100D (Inglewood-built). Pilot: Dan Darnell.

Jan 27: CDI and CTCI Boards completed F-100D inspection.

Feb 06: USAF issued letter contract AF 33 (600)-31388 authorizing production of 113 additional F-100D airplanes to be built at NAA's Columbus, Ohio, plant.

Feb 20: Completion of IR missile modifications on F-100Ds: s/n 54-2145 (ship no. 25) with GAR-2 missile; s/n 54-2138 (ship no. 18) and s/n 54-2144 (ship no. 24) with Naval Ordnance Test Station (NOTS) Sidewinder.

Two F-100Ds of the 110th TFS Missouri Air National Guard cruise over the Midwest. *Courtesy Jay Miller Aviation History Collection*

1956 Mar 02: USAF issued contract cancellation notice (CCN) authorizing production program for installation of provisions for NOTS Sidewinder on F-100D 55-3502 (ship no. 184) and subsequent at Los Angeles.

Mar 23: USAF issued CCN authorizing production program for installation of provisions for NOTS Sidewinder on F-100D s/n 55-2784 (ship no. 51) and subsequent at Columbus.

Apr: F-100C production ended.

Apr: F-100D first acceptance.

Jun 12: First flight, Columbus-built production F-100D.

Jun 14: USAF equipped the Thunderbirds aerial demonstration team with 6 F-100C models.

mid-1956: USAF considered YF-107A as potential replacement for Republic F-105; test program was accelerated.

Jul: Last F-100C accepted by USAF.

Aug 03: TF-100C (prototype of F-100F) first flight, achieved level-flight supersonic speed.

Sep 07: Basic release of 8,881 F-100F old and new engineering drawings to manufacturing. Total engineering hours expended: 236,248 (130,632 at Columbus; 105,616 at Los Angeles).

Sep: F-100D deliveries began to TAC units at Langley AFB, Virginia.

Sep 10: First flight, first prototype YF-107A.

Sep 19: F-100Cs out of Foster AFB made trans-Atlantic deployment to Landstuhl Air Base, Germany, using 450-gallon fuel tanks and refueling in flight. First jet aircraft non-stop crossing of Atlantic. Code name: Project Mobile Baker. Flight time: 13 hours 30 minutes.

Sep 29: F-100D entered operational service with 405th Fighter-Bomber Wing (FBW), Langley AFB.

Oct 12: USAF issued CCN authorizing production program for incorporation of ZEL (zero-length launch) capabilities in last 148 F-100D aircraft.

1957 Jan 07: First F-100F completed by factory, on schedule.

Feb: F-107 program discontinued.

Mar 06: CDI and CTCI Boards completed F-100F inspection.

Mar 07: First flight of first production F-100F. Pilot: Al White. Achieved supersonic speed in level flight.

Mar 15: USAF issued CCN authorizing installation of ECM provisions in F-100D s/n 56-3023 (ship no. 617) and subsequent at Los Angeles, and s/n 56-3407 (ship no. 278) and subsequent at Columbus, and in F-100F s/n 56-3725 (ship no. 1) and subsequent. NAA submitted proposals for retrofits to F-100Ds back to s/n 55-3502 (ship no. 184) at Los Angeles and s/n 55-2784 (ship no. 51) at Columbus.

Mar 22: General Operating Requirement (GOR) 68 cancelled; three YF-107As transferred to NACA.

Apr 09: TF-100C spun out of control and crashed during demonstration spin testing. Chief Test Pilot Bob Baker ejected and landed without injury.

Apr 10: NAA was assigned all management responsibility for program to improve F-100 fire-control system.

Apr 24: USAF issued letter contract AF 33 (600)-35160 authorizing production of 87 additional F-100F airplanes and 13 additional F-100Ds.

May 13: Three F-100Cs set single-engine jet aircraft distance record, 6,710 miles from London to Los Angeles; time: 14 hours 5 minutes, using in-flight refueling. Average speed , 477.00 mph. Three other F-100Cs landed purposely at Jamestown, Virginia. All six launched for same purpose: to demonstrate long-range striking power of TAC.

May 17: First F-100F accepted by USAF.

May 21: F-100F s/n 56-3730 left New York on nonstop flight to Paris, commemorating 30th anniversary of Lindbergh's flight. Code name: Project Europa.

A quartet of 110th TFS Missouri Air National Guard Huns fly in formation over the Mississippi River.
Courtesy Jay Miller Aviation History Collection

Two 110th TFS Missouri Air National Guard F-100Ds sit on a ramp. *Courtesy Jay Miller Aviation History Collection*

1957 May 27: USAF issued CCN for Project Green Door, field modifications by NAA Field Service teams at USAF bases to upgrade automatic flight-control system, automatic LABS system, and G retention.

May 31: Operational training unit at Nellis AFB equipped with first supersonic trainer, F-100F.

Aug 01: USAF issued CCN against contract AF-35160 (1957 Apr 24) eliminating production of additional 13 F-100D aircraft, and reducing quantity of F-100F to 40, to be designated as F-100F-20.

Sep 01: USAF issued CCN stretching out completion of F-100D airplanes from Sep 1958 to Aug 1959, and of F-100F airplanes from Jun 1958 to Aug 1959. Rate of completion limited to 10 per month including F-100F-20, in lieu of approximately 35 airplanes per month.

Oct 30: USAF issued Amendment Number 4 to contract AF-35160 (1957 Apr 24) authorizing modification of F-100F (ship no. 163) to prototype of F-100F-20.

Dec 12: First test of ZEL system, using dummy mass, was completed at Edwards AFB.

Dec: F-100D last acceptance from Columbus.

1958 Jan 14: USAF issued CNN No. 1 to contract AF-35160, reducing quantity of F-100F-20 airplanes from 40 to 29.

Jan: F-100F first acceptance.

Feb 07: First transfer of 47 F-100As from USAF active inventory to Air National Guard (ANG); unit receiving first F-100A was 188th Fighter Interceptor Squadron, New Mexico ANG, Kirkland AFB.

Mar 26: First piloted F-100 ZEL launch made by NAA test pilot Al Blackburn.

Apr 11: Second piloted ZEL launch made, but booster rocket did not disengage. Pilot Blackburn ejected and aircraft (s/n 56-2904) was destroyed.

May 01: First Military Assistance Program (MAP) F-100F airplanes delivered to France.

A 110th TFS Missouri Air National Guard F-100D s/n 55-3770. *Courtesy Jay Miller Aviation History Collection*

1958 Jun 17: USAF issued letter contract AF-37687 authorizing production of nine additional F-100F-15 airplanes, extending production into August 1959.

Aug 07: Consolidated F-100 Project Group of 120 men formed from key individuals working in engineering design groups on F-100 systems.

Aug 29: Eighth piloted ZEL launch, first by USAF. Pilot: AFFTC Captain Titus.

Oct 01: First MAP F-100F airplane delivered to Nationalist Chinese on Formosa.

Oct 08: USAF authorized rehabilitation and compliance of four RF-100A Special Configuration Aircraft (Slick Chick).

Oct 16: First MAP F-100F delivered to Turkey.

Oct 21: First MAP F-100D delivered to Turkey.

Oct 23: Twentieth and last piloted ZEL launch successfully made.

Nov 17: USAF authorized production of six additional F-100F-15 airplanes, extending production into September 1959.

Dec 04: First F-100F-20 airplane of contract AF-35160 delivered.

Dec 22: Last F-100F airplane of contract AF-31863 delivered.

1959: MAP sent 15 F-100As to Nationalist China; TAC stored most of remainder of inventory at Nellis AFB.

May 18: First MAP F-100D airplanes delivered to France.

Aug: F-100D last acceptance from Inglewood.

Aug 7: First F-100 over the North Pole, Operation Julius Caesar.

1960: Additional 65 F-100As sent to Nationalist China; full quota of 70 F-100As in service with ANG.

1961: Four F-100As equipped with reconnaissance equipment ("Slick Chick" aircraft) and designated RF-100A. Delivered to Nationalist China late in year under Military Assistance Program.

1961: Forty-seven major accidents, modifications, and cannibalizing accounted for phase-out of entire remaining active fleet of F-100A.

1961:	Berlin Crisis; call-up of Air National Guard and Air Force Reserve units with F-100s.	**1965 Nov 21:**	Four Wild Weasel F-100Fs deployed from Eglin AFB, Florida, to Korat RTAFB, Thailand, assigned to operational control of 388th TFW.
early 1962:	USAF decided to extend F-100 service life; many ANG F-100s kept in TAC inventory after personnel released.	**Dec 03:**	First Wild Weasel missions flown.
		1966 Feb 27:	Three more Wild Weasel aircraft deployed to Southeast Asia.
May:	Initial deployment of F-100s from 13th AF to Thailand.	**early 1970:**	USAF retired last F-100A, three years after ANG had lost remaining few through attrition.
Jun:	First F-100s arrived in Southeast Asia, although it wasn't until 1965 that they flew their first combat missions over Vietnam.	**1972 Jun 19:**	Last F-100 in TAC retired.
1964 Jul:	Thunderbirds re-equipped with F-100D models.	**1979 Nov 10:**	Last F-100 in AF/ANG retired.

Notice the discoloration of the afterburner section on this French F-100D s/n 54-2165. *Courtesy David W. Menard*

INDEX

3rd TFW, 84
8th TFW, 89
12th TFS, 89
31st TFW, 70
39th Air Division, 75
110th TFS, 73, 85
116th TFS, 88
118th TFS, 43
131st Fighter Squadron (FS), 89
188th TFS, 83
307th TFS, 70
366th TFW, 89
388th TFW, 89
401st TFW, 79
428th TFS, 73, 89
429th TFS, 45, 85
430th TFS, 88
478th TFS, 71, 85
479th FDW, 15, 42, 44
481st TFS, 86
510th TFS, 84
531st TFW, 87
4758th Defense Systems Evaluation Squadron, 49

A4 gun sight, 67–70, 73, 74
AA-1 missiles, 51
afterburner, 23
AGM-12B Bullpup missile system, 69–72, 75
AGM-45 radar-homing seeker, 72
Aircraft
    707 airliner, 21
    B-47, 37
    B-52 Stratofortress, 21, 87
    D-558-1 Skystreak, 15
    D-571, 15
    DC-8, 21
    F-3H-1 Demon, 17
    F-4 Phantom II, 79, 83, 88, 89
    F4D-1 Skyray, 10, 16, 17
    F-16, 79
    F-84G, 77
    F-86 Sabre, 9, 10, 12, 14, 23, 35
    F-86D Sabre Dog, 10, 14
    F-86E Sabre, 10
    F-86F Sabre, 63
    F-100A, 11, 13–15, 24, 29, 37, 38, 40–43, 45, 47, 53, 54, 59, 67, 69, 73, 80, 91–93
    F-100B, 53, 63, 75, 91–93, 98
    F-100C, 14, 33, 34, 37, 41, 43–45, 47, 49, 53–56, 58–60, 63, 67, 72, 73, 79
    F-100D, 14, 33, 45, 47, 48, 51, 53, 55–58, 60, 62, 63, 66, 70, 72–75, 77–82, 84–87, 100, 101
    F-100F, 33, 45, 48, 50, 53, 58–60, 66, 72, 75–77, 79, 80, 85, 86, 88, 89

F-101 Voodoo, 21
F-102 Delta Dagger, 21
F-105 Thunderchief, 87, 98, 91
F-105D, 96
F-105G, 88
F-107A, 90, 91, 93, 94–98
FW 757, 41
I-360 prototype, 17
KC-135A, 48
MiG-17, 83
MiG-19, 15–19, 50, 51
MiG-21, 83
MIGCAP, 83
P-51 Mustang, 9, 16
P-51D, 77
QF-100D, 72
RF-100A "Slick Chick," 80, 100, 101
SM-1/2, 17
SM-2, 17
SM-9/1, 17
TF-100F, 79
U-2, 84, 86
X-15, 99
XF4D-1 Skyray, 15, 16, 19, 50
XJ53, 10
XS-1, 9, 13
YF-100, 10–12, 17, 35
YF-100A, 14, 35–37, 50, 53
YF-105, 98
AIM-9 Sidewinder missile, 51, 68–70, 72, 75, 80
Air Force Flight Test Center (AFFTC), 35, 36
Air Force Museum, 97, 100
Allison, 17
AN/AJB bombing system, 74, 75
AN/AJB-1B, 75
AN/AJB-5A, 75
AN/APG 30 radar system, 67, 73
AN/APR-25 radar receiver, 86
AN/APR-26 receiver, 86
AN/APS-54 radar, 80
AN/APX-6 identification radar, 13
AN/ARC-34 UHF radio set, 13
AN/ARN-6 radio compass, 13
AN/ASE-17 radar system, 68
AN/ASG-17 radar system, 73
Applied Technology, Inc. (ATI), 85, 86
APR-25 RHAW system, 86, 87
Apt, Mel, 38
Arado, 9
Armée de l'air, See French Air Force
AS-2 missile, 83
Atwood, lee, 9, 98

B28 nuclear weapon, 72
B43 nuclear weapon, 72
B57 nuclear weapon, 72

B61 nuclear weapon, 72
Baker, Bob, 37, 98
Barnes, Commander Colonel William F., 36
Bell, 9, 13
Bien Hoa Air Base, 70, 84
Boeing, 21, 37
Brooks Air Force Base, 60

Central Intelligence Agency (CIA), 80
Central Jutland Peninsula, 77
Châteauroux, 81
Chinese Nationalist Air Force (CNAF), 79, 80
Clark Air Base, 83
cockpit, 26–31
Collier trophy, 50
combustors, 22, 23
Communist Party, Central Committee of, 17
Convair, 21
Cook, Gen. Orval R., 14
Cook-Craigie Plan, 13, 14
Council of Ministers, 17
Craigie, Gen. Laurence C., 14
Crossfield, Scott, 99, 100

Darnell, Daniel, 36
Davis-Monthan Air Force Base, 79
Day, Major George, 88
Dempster Task Force, 85
Dempster, Brigadier General K. C., 84, 85
Det Kongelige Danske Flyvevaben (DKDF), See Royal Danish Air Force
Directive No. 286-133, 17
Douglas Aircraft Company, 10, 15, 17, 21, 50

Edwards Air Force Base, 12, 35, 50, 98
Eglin Air Force Base, 87
Elektron castings, 17
Engineering Study Order (ESP) 713, 91
Engines
    40-WE-8, 50
    J35, 10, 17, 22
    J40, 10, 16, 17, 22
    J47, 10, 22
    J48, 10
    J57, 11, 13, 16, 17, 19, 21, 22, 23, 24, 25, 56, 91, 92, 95
    J75, 92, 92, 94–96, 99
    JT3, 21
    JT4, 96
    Klimov RD-9B turbojets, 17–19, 51
    YJ75-P-11, 95
England Air Force Base, 87
Erhac, Malatya, 79
Escadre 11, 81
Eskadrille (ESK), 77, 78
Eskisehir, 79

Everest, Lieutenant Colonel Frank K. (Pete) Jr., 35–37, 50

flaps, 25
flight-control hydraulic system, 26
Flyvertaktisk Kommando, 77
Focke-Wulfe, 9
Ford Aerospace Tiger Claws, 67
French Air Force, 80, 81
fuselage, 23

Gate of Skrydstrup, 79
General Dynamics, 79
General Electric, 10, 22, 63
General Electric, Pontiac Division, 63, 64, 67
General Motors, Allison Division, 10
George Air Force Base, 15

Hartman, Richard, 85
Heinemann, Ed, 15–17, 50
Heinkel, 9
Homestead Air Force Base, 87
horizontal stabilizer, 24, 25
hydraulic power system, 25

Illinois Institute of Technology, 64
inertia roll coupling, 38–41
intake, 23
IR-133 radar warning receiver, 86, 87
Iron Hand unit, 87
IXA pylon, 69

Jaguar, 81
Johnson, Richard, 36

KA-60 camara, 86
Karup, 77
Kindelberger, James H., 50
Konya, 79
Korat Royal Thai Air Force Base, 87
KUS-1000 indicator, 19

LAU-3 canister, 87
Lippisch, Alexander, 15
Lockheed, 84, 86
Los Angeles International Airport, 14
Luke Air Force Base, 87
Lynch, Joseph, 36

M1 bombing system, 74
M39 cannon, 63–66
M39E cannon, 67
M61 Vulcan "Gatling gun," 67
MA12 fire-control system, 96
MA2 bombing system, 74, 75
Massachusetts Air National Guard, 89
Masserschmitt, 9

Mauser MG213C gun, 64
McClellen Air Force Base, 52
McDonnell, 17, 21, 79, 83
McKay, John, 99
McPeak, Capt. "Tony," 58
Messerschmitt Me-163 interceptor, 15
Misawa Air Base, 75
Missouri Air National Guard, 73, 85
MJ1 "Jammer," 70
MK7 nuclear weapon, 72
Myrtle Beach Air Force Base, 87

NAS North Island, 19
National Advisory Committee on Aeronautics (NACA), 9, 12, 41, 99
NATO 4th Allied Tactical Air Force, 80
Nellis Air Force Base, 59, 74, 87
New Mexico Air National Guard, 83
North American Aviation (NAA), 9–17, 35–38, 41, 50, 53–55, 58, 59, 86, 91, 92, 98, 99, 101
North American Aviation, Long Beach Special Operations Unit, 86

Ohio Air National Guard, 88, 89
Operational Conversion Unit, 78

Pearl Harbor, 35
performance, testing, 41–51
Peterson, Forrest, 99
Pima Air Museum, 100
Pogue, Bud, 37
powerplant, 21, 22
Powers, Francis Gary, 84
Pratt & Whitney, 10, 11, 13, 19, 21, 22, 53, 56, 92, 94, 96
Pratt, Francis, 21
Pratt, Perry W., 21

Rahn, Robert, 50
Republic Aviation, 77, 87, 91, 96, 98
Republic of China Air Force (ROCAF), 80
Rice, Raymond H., 9, 11, 41
Rogers Dry Lake, 36, 90, 98
Rolls-Royce, 10
Root, Gene, 15
Rover, 10
Royal Danish Air Force, 76–79

SA-2 missile, 84–86
SAAB, 78
Salton Sea, 50
Sandelius, Captain Edward E., 87
Skrydstrup, 77
Slick Chick, See RF-100A
Smith, A. M. O., 15
Smith, R. G., 15

speed brakes, 25
Strategic Air Command, 87

T-130 cannon, 12
T160 gun, 63
Tactical Air Command (TAC), 37, 87
Texas Air National Guard, 62
THK Filo, 79
TP-260 receiver, 19
Tsagi flaps, 17
Turk Hava Kuvvetleri (THK), See Turkish Air Force
Turkish Air Force, 79
Tuy Hoa Air Base, 83

U.S. Air Force, 10–12, 15, 25, 36, 37, 41, 50, 53, 58, 79, 80, 83, 84, 101
U.S. Air National Guard, 79
U.S. Navy Bureau of Aeronautics (BUAER), 15
U.S. Navy, 15, 17, 21
U.S. Tactical Air Command, 77
utility hydraulic system, 25, 26

VAID program, 99
VD-20 altimeter, 19
Vector IV radar homing and warning system, 72
Verdin, Lt. Comdr. James, 50

Welch, George, 8, 35–38
Westinghouse, 10, 16, 21, 22, 50
Westmoreland, Gen. William C., 84
White, Bob, 99
White, Captain Edward B., 87
Wild Weasel configuration, 72, 83–90
Willgoos, Andy, 21
World War II, 9, 16, 64
Wright Air Development Center (WADC), 36
Wright-Patterson Air Force Base, 97, 100

Yeager, Charles E., 9

Other **Zenith Press** titles of interest to the enthusiast:

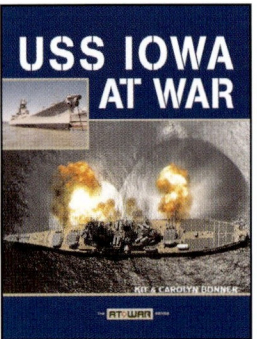

USS Iowa at War
978-0-7603-2804-0
0-7603-2804-8

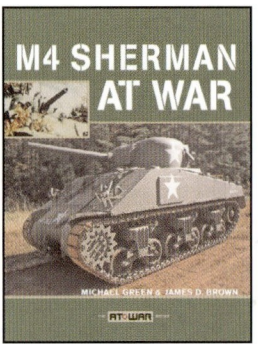

M4 Sherman at War
978-0-7603-2784-5
0-7603-2784-X

B-17 at War
978-0-7603-2522-3
0-7603-2522-7

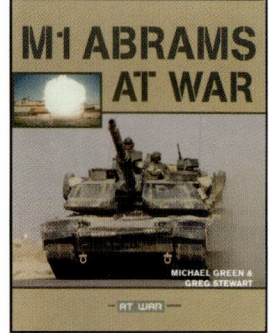

M1 Abrams at War
978-0-7603-2153-9
0-7603-2153-1

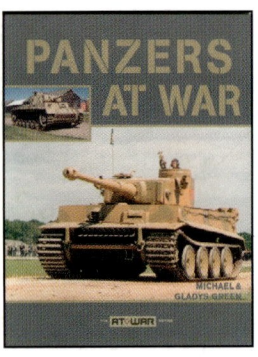

Panzers at War
978-0-7603-2152-2,
0-7603-2152-3

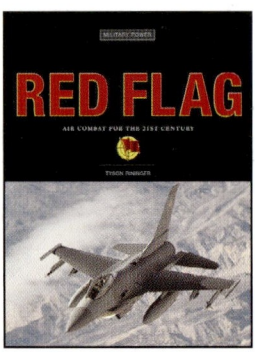

Red Flag
978-0-7603-2530-8
0-7603-2530-8

U.S. Air Force Special Ops
978-0-7603-2947-4
0-7603-2947-8

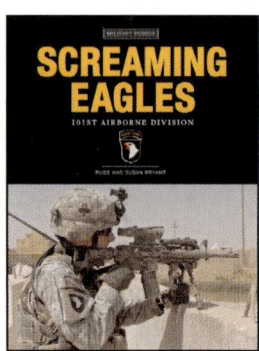

Screaming Eagles
978-0-7603-3122-4
0-7603-3122-7

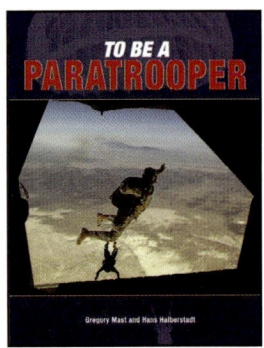

To Be a Paratrooper
978-0-7603-3046-3
0-7603-3046-8

ZENITH PRESS

Find us on the internet at
www.zenithpress.com or
call **1-800-826-6600**

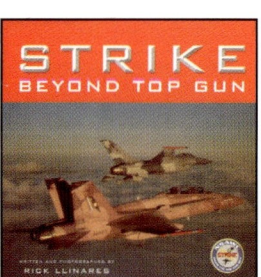

Strike: Beyond Top Gun
978-0-7603-2525-4
0-7603-2525-1